VIRTUAL BODY LANGUAGE

The History and Future of Avatars: How
Nonverbal Expression is Evolving on the
Internet

Jeffrey Ventrella

Ventrella, Jeffrey, J.

Virtual Body Language – The History and Future of Avatars:
How Nonverbal Expression is Evolving on the Internet

Book web site: www.virtualbodylanguage.com

Copyright © 2011 by Jeffrey Ventrella

ISBN: 978-1-257-76355-9

Library of Congress Control Number: 2011929759

Published by ETC Press
http://etc.cmu.edu/etcpress/

Design & composition by Jeffrey Ventrella
Cover art by Jeffrey Ventrella

A Note on Punctuation

I have adopted the British style of placing punctuation that is not part of a quoted phrase *outside* the quotation marks, because the American convention is based on a historical accident. And Lynne Truss, author of *Eats, Shoots & Leaves*, thinks it's silly. Lynne Truss totally ROCKS, and so I dedicate my civil disobedience to her. With apologies to my American sticklers in punctuation, I hope you don't mind that I have adopted the more logical convention for typographical body language.

Also, in this book I have decided to occasionally pepper my text with members of a new species of punctuation, born on the internet. I sometimes use smileys as terminators, in place of commas or periods (I am especially fond of using smileys at the ends of parenthetical statements :)

Contents

1	Faux Pas of an Unattended Avatar	7
2	Body Language Goes Online	16
3	From Microbes to Post-Humans	34
4	Avatar-Centric Communication	56
5	A Body Language Alphabet	92
6	The Uncanny Valley of Expression	115
7	The Gestural Turing Test	125
8	The Tail Wagging the Brain	139
9	Verbal Ectoplasm	162
10	The Three-Dimensional Music of Gaze	177
11	Seven Hundred Puppet Strings	206
12	Voice as Puppeteer	231
13	Looking Ahead	246
Appendix:	A Manifesto of Avatar Expression	258
References		262

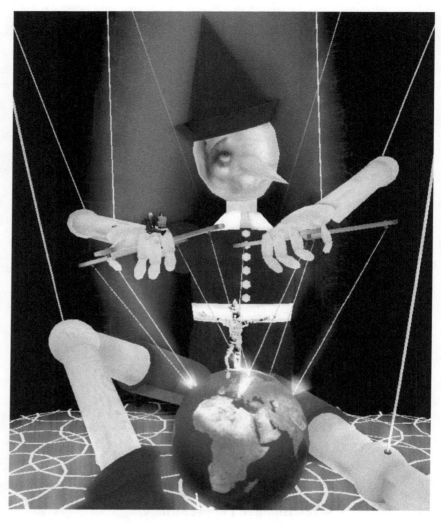

Virtual Pinocchio sculpture by Arcana Jasma (Image: Arcana Jasma)

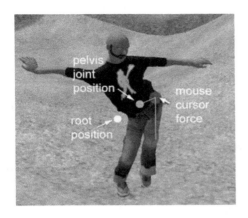

Acknowledgements

I would like to thank my wife Nuala for her patience and love, and my mom and the memory of my dad who encouraged a creative life.

I want to thank my primary editor, Claudia L'Amoreaux, whose experience in virtual worlds, technology in education, and overall scholarship provided valuable guidance. Thanks to my initial editor Nanou Matteson for a great start. Thanks to David Harrison who provided sage editing advice. A big thank you to Drew Davidson of ETC Press for helping get this book in shape for publication.

I would like to thank Will Harvey who supported me in my early years of avatar development. Thanks to Chuck Clanton, a critical creative contributor to There.com's avatar system. I would like to thank other There.com innovators such as Don Carson, Matt Danzig, Mel Guymon, Amy-Jo Kim, Tom Melcher, Janis Nakano-Spivack, Fernando Pais, Ko Patel, and the many other creative and technical contributors to the avatar system.

A big thanks for Celia Pearce for reviewing the book and giving great editing advice, and great ideas on future avatar systems. A huge thanks to Lionel Kearns for his mix of kindness and wisdom, and his ideas on language. I want to give a very special thank you to Jeremy Owen Turner who provided great friendship and advice on the SkyTrain, and hung by me during some difficult times. Thanks to Gerri Sinclair, an inspiration for those of us working at the intersection of industry and academics. Thanks to Mary Austin for suggestions on typography, layout, and visual flow. Much thanks goes out to the friends and colleagues who read drafts of the manuscript and provided valuable feedback, including Bob Moore, Richard Koman, Ryan Nadel, Catherine Winters, Andrea Romeo, Jim Vogel, and Camp Wilson. Thanks to Magy Seif El-Nasr who invited me to join her research team at the School of Interactive Art and Technology at Simon Fraser University in BC.

Thanks to my colleagues at Linden Lab: Philip Rosedale, Corey Ondrejka, Andrew Meadows, Richard Nelson, Melinda Green, Samantha Patterson, Qube, Qarl, Robin Harper, and many others who provided technical and creative help in the avatar puppeteering system. I want to thank several individuals who have provided creative support, ideas, and love throughout many years of my life, including my dear friend Gary Walker, and my brother Michael Ventrella who provided sound advice on birthing my first book. Thanks also to Brian Rotman, Wagner James Au, Jodey Castricano, Bruce Damer, Anthony Steed, Jim Bizzocchi, Eddie Elliot, Steve DiPaola, Douglas Gayeton, Joanna Robinson, Coolnet There, David Burton, Henry Lowood, and Reuben Steiger. Thanks to Portico Bowman for her ongoing encouragement and advice.

Finally, I would like to thank Brian Turko, founder of Turk's Coffee Lounge on Commercial Drive in Vancouver BC, for the best coffee in the solar system, wild music, and creative people who gather to share dreams and ambitions.

1

Faux Pas of an Unattended Avatar

Catherine was one of the most popular residents in a new virtual world that had just come onto the scene. She was creative, friendly, and entrepreneurial. She was quite attractive, and she was good at programming various aspects of her little piece of the world. But soon after she had established herself, Catherine started to get a bad reputation: people were calling her a snob.

image: Catherine Winters

This surprised Catherine, who had always made a point to be friendly to all the residents. Despite extra attempts at being sociable, Catherine's reputation continued. Then one day she overheard one of the new residents talking about her: "That Catherine—she's a snob. I had just gotten set up with my new account, and I decided to go find her, and introduce myself. As soon as I introduced myself, she turned her head to look at me, stared at me for a while without saying a word, and then turned her head back, like I wasn't even there. How rude!"

At first it was a mystery. Catherine had no recollection of ever snubbing a newbie. She would never act this way in person, nor would she act this way in a virtual world. But eventually, Catherine figured out what was going on.

The virtual world I am describing is Second Life, and the woman is Catherine Winters (avatar name, *Catherine Omega*). When she enters into this virtual world she takes the form of an *avatar*—a digital character that represents her embodiment. The software engineers at Linden Lab, makers of Second Life, designed the system so that avatars would automatically respond to the utterances of other avatars by turning their heads towards them. This was meant to make the avatars appear more natural—after all, in the real world, people usually look at each other when they are talking. But there is one problem with this notion: Second Life is not the real world. In fact, it is very different! Let me explain.

Here is a typical scenario to describe what was happening: Catherine was logged into Second Life, chatting away with other avatars, and doing the various things that people—as avatars—do in Second Life. Then Catherine (the real woman) stepped away from her computer for a moment, while Catherine (her avatar) was still standing there among other avatars. An unsuspecting newbie walked her avatar up to Catherine's avatar and started chatting. Since the real Catherine was not present to respond with a chat, her avatar looked over at the new avatar (because of the automatic avatar "lookat" behavior). Then, because there was no communication coming from Catherine, her avatar's lookat mode timed-out, and resumed its usual gaze at nothing in particular. Catherine's bad reputation, it turns out, resulted from Catherine not being there. Her avatar was generating unintended body language in her absence.

Catherine, it seems, was already prone to this kind of virtual faux pas. Even though she was chatty in general, she rarely triggered avatar animations or used smileys and other visual signs of expression. Her responses tended to be short, and spaced apart in time. The reason for this is not readily apparent unless you know her personally: Catherine's mind is like a rotating mirror ball. She typically has several instant messaging channels going at once, and is always bouncing around between simultaneous conversations. She would be the perfect poster child for the ills of Continuous Partial Attention, were it not for the fact that she is a clever blogger and self-aware master of the internet. She deftly taps the pluralistic, fragmented, connectionist intelligence of the internet, fully aware of its nature.

So, the problem lies not with the fragmented attention of Catherine the woman, but with the apparent continuous attention of Catherine the avatar. The problem of presence in virtual worlds has been researched by such scholars as Ralph Schroeder, editor of *The Social Life of Avatars* (2002), who uses the term "copresence" to describe not just "being there" but "being there together". This is the locus of virtual body language.

Mediated Selves

Am I suggesting that Catherine should be more attentive to her avatar? No—that would go against the nature of avatarhood. Most would agree that users want some form of detachment. It takes a lot of time and energy to be a fulltime puppeteer, and most people would rather not be encumbered by this job. The avatar stands as a persistent external persona that allows the user to privately engage in a hundred distractions—to be sloppy, erratic, timid, anxious, or confused, or perhaps amused, sarcastic, and snickering. Or, in Catherine's case, just plain busy. The avatar allows the user to step away for a "bio-break". The avatar is also a way for people to express their multiple personalities, sometimes even having several avatars in-world simultaneously. While having different identities has always been a part of human social life, as highlighted by sociologist Erving Goffman in the 1950's, the phenomenon has increased due to the prevalence of new media. Sherry Turkle, author of *Life on the Screen* (1995), points out that our natural multiple personalities are easily expressed and manifested in cyberspace.

Jim Bumgardner, creator of the early virtual world, The Palace, was inspired by Scott McCloud's concept of "masking" in comics (1993). Avatars, according to Bumgardner, allow users to maintain partial anonymity. This partial anonymity allows people to relax and become more expressive and creative in their interactions.

The Identity Leash

How we design avatar systems—and how people use them— determines where the avatar lies on a continuum of control. The low-end of the continuum is mostly hands-off (the avatar is semi-autonomous). The high-end of the continuum is detailed, focused control (the user is a full-time puppeteer). Early avatar-maker Steve DiPaola refers to this continuum as the "identity leash". With avatars, "…identity itself is a dynamic construct that, like a leash, can be pulled in tight or given generous slack. In this way, one does not have to choose between the extremes of either playing a role or strictly being oneself, but instead can meander through identity space of this role of the self" (DiPaola 2000). A long identity leash means that the avatar has lots of autonomy. It's allowed to do things that don't represent what the user is doing from moment to moment. A short leash means that the avatar is being puppeteered with high focus and attention. Both short and long identity leashes are appropriate for different purposes and at different times. And these modes are actually reflected in our minds as we shift focus and attention from moment to moment.

10

Catherine prefers a long identity leash. It allows her to engage in various private activities offscreen, to still be herself, and not have to share her every twitch, her every glance, and those snickering side comments with her IM buddies. It allows her to be somewhat removed, but still maintain a perpetual proxy of herself in virtual space that she occupies on a part-time basis.

Hybrid Spaces

Let's imagine that Catherine's avatar had NO gaze behavior, and never turned its head in response to another avatar's chat. On the one hand, her avatar would be boring and antisocial. But on the other hand, her avatar would not be in danger of giving false or ambiguous signals.

Now let's step back for a moment and consider something peculiar. Catherine's avatar responds to another avatar's chats by shifting its gaze to that avatar's head. Text chat in Second Life is normally configured to appear somewhere near the bottom of the screen, in a rectangular text area.

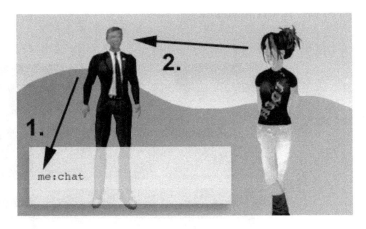

Chat appearing in text window causes gaze reaction in 3D world (Image: Ventrella)

So, wouldn't it make more sense for Catherine's avatar to set its gaze on the actual stimulus? Shouldn't her avatar look at that 2D text window where the chats are coming in?

I'm asking this question, not because I think avatars should look at incoming lines of text, but simply to point out an ambiguity in the visual scene: a semi-realistic humanoid avatar makes a semi-realistic response (turning the head in response to some stimulus)… but the response is to a completely disembodied event (the creation of a text chat in an arbitrary 2D location on a computer screen). There is something wrong with this picture!

Most prominent virtual worlds incorporate the technologies of chat rooms, instant messaging, textual conversations. We have a collision: computergraphical humanoid 3D models with text-chat. These are strange bedfellows—occupying different cognitive dimensions. This is illustrated in the screenshot below of the early virtual world, Cybertown. I had noticed earlier in such worlds that people engaged in communication tend to keep their eyes focused on the text, and rarely glance up to the 3D scene. All the interesting action seems to be going on in Text Land, while the avatars stand idly like statues in a surreal wax museum.

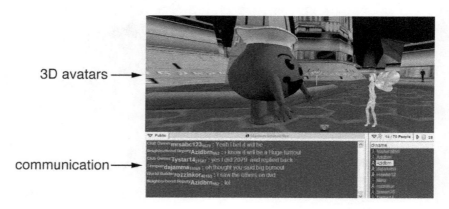

3D avatar space contrasted with text communication space in Cybertown (Image: Mark McGuire)

The avatars in the late virtual world, There.com, were able to send visual symbols (*moodicons*) back and forth to each other. It was a way to bring some embodied communication into the avatar space. But the way users typically triggered these visual expressions was by way of text, or "emotes", such as :) or 'shrug, which would appear in their chat balloons along with their normal text. But even if the user was not using text to generate these moodicons, the text would still appear in the chat balloons. WTF? So, you end up with the following strange scenario:

Generating *moodicons* causes redundant chat balloon text in There.com (Image: Jeremy Owen Turner)

One might argue that these convergent media collisions are the basis of innovation—and that the real solutions are yet to come. Let's agree on one thing: the solutions to avatar interaction design will not be arrived at simply through a better understanding of human social behavior, as some might naïvely assume. It will require an understanding of the uses and constraints of these colliding technologies. Persson (2003) points out that avatar nonverbal communication doesn't even have to be synchronous—in other words, instead of you and me expressing visually in realtime, our expressions can be sent in chunks separated by arbitrary spans of time. With asynchronous communication (Twitter, Facebook, email, etc.), users are not compelled to respond to each other at natural conversational rates. The modality of asynchronous communication permits users to customize nonverbal avatar animations with the same degree of care and craft as they might compose their emails and blog posts.

Thus, virtual body language may just as naturally arise within the scattered temporal cracks of our busy lives, being folded into similar timeslices as our text-based communications. Time is fragmented. But so is *presence*—those bits and pieces of identity and attention that accumulate in the nooks and crannies of the internet. It's a paradigm shift: "…once one accepts the state of distributed presence, inevitably this means acceptance of a group consciousness, which itself shifts our perception of time and even productivity (Vesna 2004).

Help, I'm Lost And I Have No Pants

Verhulsdonck and Morie (2009) make a call for developing nonverbal communication standards in virtual worlds, yet they acknowledge that the range of communication affordances in virtual worlds causes confusion, and so these standards will have to evolve along with the technology. The technology we're talking about is a cobbled hybrid mashup of computer games, cinema, texting, 3D rendering, and physical simulation. And the *cloud* (Boellstorff 2010). It is in a fledgling state. It has not yet been fully calibrated to our human natures and lifestyles. Catherine's faux pas, and its underlying cause, has a solution. We just haven't worked it out yet.

Susan Woita was a Customer Service employee at There.com. She recalls having to help users with some pretty strange problems. She had intended to write a book about her experiences, but never got around to it. That book was going to be called, *Help, I'm Lost and I Have No Pants!! — Real Life in a Virtual World.* That quote is verbatim from a message she got from a newbie. Her job was to find out why the pants were missing from his avatar. Turns out, he sold them to a scammer, and somehow didn't make the connection between that interaction and the fact that his pants were missing (Woita 2010).

In virtual reality, whether or not someone has just taken off your pants is not always obvious. The fact that gravity pulls things downward is not always a given. That has to be programmed. Or not. Internet visionary Ted Nelson sees today's computer world as "...a nightmare honkytonk prison, noisy and colorful and wholly misbegotten" (2008). That is both a cause for anxiety and a cause for celebration. *That* is the honkytonk origin of avatars and virtual worlds.

Segue

What follows is a stroll through the philosophical, sociological, aesthetic, neurological, and technical consequences of having a virtual body...and communicating with that body. In this book I will be exploring many forms of virtual body language that have sprung up. And I will make some predictions about what body language might look like in the future. I will also propose a few novel solutions to the emerging challenges.

Even if you are not a computer geek, gamer, technologist, media theorist, or internet junkie, you *are* fascinated with the human body and how it works. And that's because you *have one*. And you *communicate with it*. Now let's forge ahead, and look at what happens when body language goes online.

2

Body Language Goes Online

Let's do a thought experiment. Imagine that you have invited a friend over for dinner—someone you know really well who is an engaging conversational partner. Your friend arrives, and you choose a favorite topic and start chatting. Easy enough. But here's the tricky part: you and your friend both have to sit motionless while talking. You are not allowed to make any facial expressions. No moving your head around, no hand gestures…nothing (other than what is absolutely necessary for speech). You may blink your eyes to keep them from drying out, but not for expression. Gaze straight ahead. Do not look at each other. Do not shift in your chair. Do not crack a smile. You may move your jaw, lips, tongue, diaphragm and throat muscles in order to generate the sounds of speech. But that's all. It sounds difficult, doesn't it?

There's another way to find out what it's like to talk in a body that has no body language: log into a virtual world that features a voice chat system. Start speaking into your computer microphone, then see and hear what happens. Depending on the virtual world you are using, you might experience something similar to what I have just described. In fact you may feel a bit like a propped-up corpse with a telephone speaker attached to its head. This corpse-effect could be alleviated by using the avatar animation features available in some virtual worlds, or by utilizing an *automatic gesticulation feature* (such as the one I created for Second Life that uses the sound of your voice to generate arm and head movements in your avatar—more on that later). But these features would only alleviate the problem a bit, and that's because avatar animations and automatic gesticulation systems are not sophisticated enough to handle the subtlety of expressive movement that accompanies speech.

Still, avatars are amazing things. And the flock of virtual worlds that came into being over the past few decades has created a lot of buzz about them—not only among computer gaming and virtual world enthusiasts, but increasingly, universities and research labs are taking an interest. One reason is that there are currently several hundred million registered users of virtual worlds (Engage Digital 2009). A recent estimate puts it at one billion (Watters 2010). Many of these registered users are choosing to live significant fractions of their lives as avatars.

The word "avatar" was first used to denote the graphical representation of a user, in *Habitat*, the online role playing game created in the mid '80s by Randy Farmer and Chip Morningstar for Lucasfilm. Below are a few early screenshots from *Habitat*, from a 1986 article in Compute! magazine (Yakal 1986).

Early screenshots from *Habitat* (image © 1986, LucasArts Entertainment)

From these crude beginnings, avatars have come a long way in terms of realism (as indicated by the picture of Catherine at the beginning of the last chapter). But they are still clunky when it comes to realtime nonverbal expression. This is one reason why many scholars are focusing attention on the avatar: as a new medium of communication, the avatar has some behavioral issues, social problems, low EQ, *autism spectrum disorders*, and the like. The avatar needs help, and it has scholars scratching their heads.

Most people, given the choice, would rather have their remote conversations using text chat, telephone, or video chat, rather than enter into an online virtual world as an avatar—even if that avatar is built for communication. I am one of those people, despite the fact that for over six years I was co-founder and Principle Inventor of There.com, an online virtual world that featured avatar expression, and later, I was a developer on *Second Life*. More recently, I worked at Simon Fraser University researching nonverbal communication in avatars (Ventrella et al. 2010)(Isbister et al. 2010)(Seif El-Nasr et al. 2011). My nearly ten years in the virtual worlds industry and related academic research is not based on a love for gaming and cyberspace, or a desire to virtualize my life. It is based on the recognition that this communication medium is young and fertile, and it has a long way to go, particularly for conducting virtual body language.

Definitions

Before delving any further, I want to first give a few definitions, so that we have some grounding in terminology. *Body language* consists of postures, hand gestures, facial expressions, eye contact, head movements, and voice intonations. These non-verbal channels of communication reveal physical, mental, and emotional states, and much of it is unconscious—both to the sender and the receiver. To be accurate, "body language" is really not a proper *natural language*, such as Chinese or Navajo, but rather, a *subset* of *natural language*. Or, depending on your point of view, you might consider it to be a *superset* of natural language. After all, body language predates human natural language...by a few billion years (depending on how you define "body" and how you define "language").

Throughout this book, "body language" should be taken to mean all nonverbal signaling, movements, and expressions, separate from the utterance of words. Furthermore, body language *may* or *may not* accompany the utterance of words. The word "paralanguage" is sometimes used to denote the full range of communication channels, usually in connection with speech. The anthropologist Ray Birdwhistell coined the term "kinesics" (1970) to refer to the interpretation, science, or study of body language. *Prosody*, the musicality of speech, is an important channel of body language.

The term *body language* is also sometimes used to refer to "static" visual attributes of a person, projected though clothing, hair, jewelry, physique, and other accoutrements that express persona, status, culture, mood, and attitude. This is an important and well-studied aspect of social signaling, but it is not the focus in this book: this book is concerned primarily with the dynamic aspects of nonverbal communication—how we express through movement.

The field of *gesture studies* is very active. There are several recommended books on the subject (such as Adam Kendon's, *Gesture: Visible Action as Utterance* (2004)).

Natural Language Deficit

What is happening to human communication as it goes online? Answer: it is getting the cold shoulder. Sandy Pentland, in *Honest Signals*, suggests that our communication technologies treat people like "cogs in an information-processing machine", and he suggests that this is based on society's infatuation with the *rational human*. But human communication is always socially and emotionally situated. According to Pentland, attempts to remedy this problem have resulted in "interfaces that pretend to have feelings or call us by name, filters that attempt to shield us from digital onslaught, and smart devices that organize our lives by gossiping behind our backs. But the result usually feels like it was designed to keep us isolated, wandering like a clueless extra in a cold virtual world" (2008). Reminds me of what I once heard the 3D animation innovator Brad deGraf call virtual reality: "a lonely place". (Happily, it has become less lonely since he made that statement :)

The BBC published a large coffee table book called *The Human Face*, by Brian Bates, with John Cleese, to accompany a television series. Concerning new communications media, the authors warn, "...today, we are doing more and more faceless, and therefore, expressionless, communicating. E-mail and other computer-aided connections can be extremely effective adjuncts to face-to-face interaction. But business is relying on it increasingly as a medium for complex communications and negotiations. And for the young, especially, much social time is spent in 'conversation' with people who are remote geographically, and whom they have never met personally. There are advantages to this...However, we need to be more clear about what we are losing. Expressions are a potent part of our connection with one another. What are the consequences of communicating without them?" (Bates 2001)

I believe the consequences are not good. For instance, in a virtual classroom (for distance learning), there should be more than a disembodied text or voice originating from the teacher. For education to be effective, we have to capture that nuanced and magical spark from the wise men and women who are skilled at dialog and debate, fueling a sense of wonder and confidence, and showing students how to communicate with their whole bodies. Henry Jenkins, in a February, 2010 Frontline interview, said this about teaching in a virtual world: "...my gestures are an important part of who I am...That I have to think about what I'm saying and what I'm doing with my body all the time on a deeply conscious level means that I'm really restricted as a teacher. So, when I go into Second Life and give a lecture I really feel stripped down of the basic stuff that allows me as a human being to communicate with another human being" (Jenkins 2010).

Primordial Avatars

Solutions to the faceless internet are popping up all around. As we spend more time communicating with text in realtime, we appear to be compulsively inserting substitutions for nonverbal expression. It's inevitable. The *emoticon*, a kind of primordial static avatar expression, has rescued many email messages from dire misinterpretation.

:)	: (	;)	: D
smiley	frown	wink	laughing

: /	> ;)	: *	> : (
skeptical	evil grin	kiss	mad

The emoticon is a species of body language that is coevolving along with other forms, *including* the avatar—sometimes even being used to trigger avatar expressions in virtual worlds. I believe that the emoticon currently still has more leverage than the avatar: its roots are in typographical soil, an ecosystem that is much older and more established than virtual worlds. (We will come back to the subject of emoticons again later).

Video Chat

Another way we are reconstituting body language online is by video-broadcasting our expressions. Video chat is the visual counterpart to the telephone, and it is making a huge difference. But, as we will be exploring in depth throughout this book, video chat is actually *more constraining* in some ways, particularly in terms of free expressivity. It requires realtime movement of the sender's body, and is constrained to the limitations of time and space. It therefore does not qualify as a plastic language that scales up—as an *out-of-body* kind of *body language*.

Also, with video chat, many people are not physically able to generate all the movement that they would want projected to their receivers because they are tired, ill, or physically disabled. Wouldn't you love to see a bouncy, hand-flapping, facial-expressing Stephen Hawking? Right now he is trapped inside a nearly motionless body. Of course we all marvel at his textual explanations of the origins of the universe. But can we really experience the subtlety of his emotional and aesthetic motivations—what "moves" him? Can we really see how he groks the big bang…with his whole being? Watching Hawking via video chat would be moot. You may as well be watching a static picture of him while he "talks" through his personal speech synthesizer.

Virtual body language is very different than expression via video chat. Similar to the way that written language provides an encoding of verbal communications, an emerging *body language alphabet* (not yet articulated) will come into form, and enable realtime nonverbal expression on the internet. Stephen Hawking's speech synthesizer is a tiny microbe-sized glimpse of what I'm talking about.

Telekinesics

I propose the term "telekinesics" to denote the study of all emerging nonverbal practices across the internet, by adding the prefix, *tele* to

Birdwhistell's, term *kinesics*. It could easily be confused with "telekinesis": the ability to cause movement at a distance through the mind alone (the words differ by only one letter). But hey, these two phenomena are not so different anyway, so a slip of the tongue wouldn't be such a bad thing. Telekinesics may be defined as "the science of body language as conducted over remote distances via some medium, including the internet". It appears that the term, "telekinesic" has been used by Mary D. Sheridan as a way to describe body language as experienced across some physical distance, in young children and babies (1977). I propose we expand this distance via digital technology: body language can be transmitted in realtime on a global scale.

Wings

The language we humans speak is not so amazing in the context of billions of years of genetic evolution: DNA has an alphabet and a grammar of its own. Its expressive power gave rise to the biosphere, which in turn gave rise to brains, culture, and the spoken word. The evolution of the spoken word enabled culture to be transmitted at a higher rate. And when the written word was invented, speech was encoded in a more precise and portable form. It sprouted wings—puncturing the equilibrium of cultural evolution. Manifested as text, language leaped beyond the here and now—it could travel vast spaces, beyond the pocket of air and light between a group of individuals. It became plastic, infinitely expressive. And it could replicate reliably—like DNA.

But natural language did not evolve only for speaking mouths and listening ears (nor only for writing hands and reading eyes). There is a visual/physical dimension to natural language, which evolved right along with speech, and which is in fact much older than speech, as earthly languages go. We generate this visual language with our bodies—our postures, gestures, facial expressions, and gaze. And just as speech has been encoded as text, so may body language be encoded—as a kind of nonverbal text. It will sprout *nonverbal wings* and occupy an infinite space. It will become plastic. The internet is becoming more visual and interactive all the time. Body language will be reconstituted, by popular demand. The "disembodied agencies" and "lettered selves" (Rotman 2008)—anomalies of the written word—are giving way (or at least taking a less dominant role) to a new embodied communication, more compatible with the dynamic, visual medium of the internet.

The biosphere sprouts homuncular wings (Image: Ventrella)

In the picture above of the Earth I added a schematic of the *homunculus*—the map of the body in the brain (later in the book I will discuss the homunculus and its implications for virtual body language). This image illustrates the fact that virtual representations of the human body are emerging, along with other representations of embodiment, as the internet envelops the earth. This is giving rise to a new layer over the biosphere—analogous to the emergence of the neocortex of the brain.

The Business Rationale for Virtual Body Language

I'll get more down-to-earth. Consider the businessperson from Beijing who flies to North America for a 4-hour meeting, hangs out for a few days, and then flies back home. In an effort to conserve capital and reduce the human carbon footprint, we are flying less. Real meetings are being replaced with online meetings through teleconferencing, or in some cases, avatar meetups in virtual spaces.

But here's the problem: you and I know that there is nothing that can replace the chemistry of real face-to-face communication. That Beijing businessperson needs to get all the subtle cues and hints about his or her North American counterpart's unspoken agenda in order to make that ten million dollar decision. Without body language, voice intonation—even the "energy" of the furniture in the room and the energy exchanged between the background people in the room—without these important contextual references, it is hard to use one's intuitive powers to make an important decision. In a virtual setting, those fundamental non-verbal cues that we rely on would have to be encoded and distributed for deep online communication that reaches the limbic system. We designers and engineers have to do the hard work to make this happen.

But some people, like Francoise Legoues, V.P. of Innovation Initiatives of IBM, are not waiting for us to get it right. She estimates that the company has already saved over a million dollars by meeting in virtual worlds instead of physically flying to meetings. Whether or not these virtual meetings are as productive as face-to-face meetings is a huge topic for discussion. In order to answer these kinds of questions, the subtleties of face-to-face interaction among teams are now being closely examined.

In *Honest Signals*, Pentland describes the results from extensive research he and his colleagues have done in studying the unconscious social signaling in companies and teams. They used a battery-powered badge-like device called the "sociometer", worn by members of the group, which gathers multiple channels of social signaling. It includes a microphone, an accelerometer, an infrared sensor, and other hardware for measuring various social signals. These signals include face-to-face interaction, features of speech, aspects of body movement, tracking of location, and proximity of other people. It is integrated with cell phones and computers for gathering and processing data.

Their research confirms that the human social sense is very strong, and largely unconscious. The results of group decision-making are very predictable when studied using the sociometer. The increase in global business and distributed professional teams that communicate electronically puts a crimp in our ability to use our natural social sense. We have relied on our social sense throughout most of our evolution. It is critical to making group decisions, and that is one reason why this research is so important: to better understand the phenomenon so that we can design better solutions for online communication.

Virtual body language will become a key factor in the future of global business. Avatars can step in to help. Or can they? Just because two business people are controlling virtual selves in a virtual environment does not mean that they are experiencing "chemistry" or any kind of reliable honest signaling. In fact, it is completely possible for a virtual world to present affectations, decoys, distracters, and unreliable information—whether these are inserted on purpose or whether they are the result of poorly-designed interfaces. So, it would be naïve to assume that virtual worlds are truth-spaces, open and ready to be filled with honest human exchange.

What virtual worlds do afford however is a kind of embodied language. Once this communication medium has sufficiently matured, it will allow people to communicate visually and behaviorally over remote distances, and to build their own *semiotic process* within which truth-telling (and lying, and all nuances in-between) are possible— determined by how the technology is used.

Video conferencing allows us to use natural facial expressions and bodily gestures, but is limited by the physical constraints of our bodies (and the cameras that capture them). Virtual spaces on the other hand permit endless modes of expression, where embodied effects like eye-gaze, pointing, and posture manifest, and where extra-body expressive accoutrements can be synthesized and articulated as part of a virtual semiosis. Bruce Damer, author of *Avatars!* (1998), points out that video conferencing doesn't allow the participants to create the world within which they are communicating, which can generate context and meaning. Virtual worlds, on the other hand, "promote that concept of shared, created worlds and identities not tied to the real people behind the avatars" (Damer 2010). In a virtual world, I can experience you as if we were in a café, a business conference room, or a Ferris wheel. I can morph my avatar into anything imaginable in order to make a point. While video chat is literal, avatars in virtual worlds are imaginal.

The Nonverbal Babel Fish

Modern life involves interacting with people from different cultures, in person and (increasingly) online. Imagine an Egyptian and a Swede in a phone conversation. Aside from their different accents, the handicap of language translation, and the lack of familiarity with the musical aspects of each other's native language, they are also missing visual cues, which could help in disambiguation, reinforcement of message, and affirmation of understanding. Can new technology help?

The Babel fish is a species of small yellow fish featured in *The Hitchhiker's Guide to the Galaxy*, which serves as a universal translator. A Babel fish inserted into your ear translates the speech of aliens into your native language so you can understand what they are saying. "Yahoo! Babel Fish" is a web-based application for translating text across languages. Language translation via computer applications is getting easier all the time, but it is certainly not perfect. Many "Babelizers" have been created to humorously demonstrate the inadequacies of language translation systems. Do you know what happens if you take a piece of English text and translate it through many different languages, and then back into English? Carl Tashian (2000) created a web site that lets you do just that. To test out Carl's Babelizer, I entered the following quote by George Carlin: "By and large, language is a tool for concealing the truth". What I got back was this: "The language is generally dae one (automatic device of the information entrance) to hide to the truth". The familiar phrase, "I'm a little tea pot, short and stout" becomes: "They are a small POTENTIOMETER, short circuits and a beer of malzes of the tea".

There may come a day when ubiquitous and ambient computing (invisible, everywhere, and always on) will provide Babel fish-like translation with ease, on-the spot, and transparently. I was once talking to internet guru Brewster Kahle about *Esperanto*, the language developed by L. L. Zamenhof in hopes to foster peace and international understanding. I started pontificating aloud on how to grow a new language that feeds on the *wisdom of crowds* and the organic connectivity of the internet, instead of being crafted by scholarly design. I imagined a magnificent swarm of web crawlers, digesting bits and pieces of living, breathing, world languages, to breed a new hybrid universal language.

Then Brewster, in typical fashion, rotated the conversation by ninety-degrees. He told me his idea: "Take out your iPhone". We both pulled out our iPhones. He held his up to his ear and pretended that he was a Spanish speaker who wanted to talk with me. He started generating body language indicating a desire to speak. Then he started pretending that he and I both had Babel fish-like software in our iPhones, translating our speech in realtime. Here's the cool part: Brewster, *hablando Español*, and I are standing right in front of each other, so we can generate all the nonverbal language we want (and we don't have to resort to pantomiming to make up for a lack of verbal understanding, since our iPhones are translating what we are saying on the spot). This is an example of a technology that allows nonverbal communication to stay right where it was invented: in the body. And the leverage is in a sweet little mobile app that does the Babel Fishing while we stay naturally expressing in our bodies.

Keeping body language inside of our bodies makes sense when we are standing right in front of each other, but not when we are remote. And when we are *culturally remote*, some nonverbal translation probably could help. Katherine Isbister (2004) and others have proposed the use of *embodied virtual agents* for training people in nonverbal communication in intercultural contexts. Verhulsdonck (2007) has explored virtual gesturing in intercultural contexts. Culture-specific nonverbal expression applies to social virtual worlds as well— which brings us back to the main theme of this book. Imagine controlling an avatar equipped with a *nonverbal Babel fish*—allowing translation of body movements and expressions across cultures. The concept of "wearing nonverbal dialects" (analogous to *wearing* selections from a wardrobe of avatar clothes) will be explored later in the chapter, *Voice as Puppeteer*. But first let's consider some of the reasons why avatars in virtual worlds are so clunky in the first place.

Film Animated Characters Are More Expressive Than My Avatar

It's not fair. I go see a Pixar film. The characters are brilliant. They are expressive, subtle, ironic, scary, dramatic, commanding, sexy, smart, rhetorical, and persuasive. I go home, log into a virtual world, and become an avatar. There I stand. Stiff, awkward me. Fumbling, unexpressive. Why can't I be more expressive? I am a real person, after all.

The illustration below shows some screenshots of Flash animations I created for SheZoom (shezoom.com), a woman-focused social networking website. These are from a series of avatar-expression-like mini-movies called "shemoticons"—an idea conceived of by SheZoom founder Stacey Artandi (top: "We need to talk", below that: "Work it", bottom-left: "It's a *girl* thing"). Compare these zoomy ladies to the two avatars at the bottom-right of the illustration, chatting in Second Life.

Contrasting expressiveness in *Shemoticons* to avatars in Second Life (top and left images: SheZoom; bottom-right image: Ventrella)

Why can't I be as expressive as my feisty little SheZoom characters when I'm using my avatar? Well, first of all, there is a major difference between puppeteering yourself on the spot versus having all the time in the world to craft your character's expressions ahead of time, as I did with these SheZoom characters. Such contrasting modes of "acting" are described in the book, *Acting for Animators* [Hooks, 2003].

But besides this obvious constraint, there is an absence of technology for avatar body language puppetry in virtual worlds, and a case of socially-illiterate software. Virtual World software is generally good at replicating visual appearances. And since graphics hardware is getting ever more powerful, soon the polygons used to render my avatar will become so numerous and small that they will be as small as the pixels on my screen—almost no visual artifacts will remain. Visual realism in computer games and virtual environments continues on a healthy trajectory. But behavioral realism is still lagging behind. Norm Badler of the University of Pennsylvania and others have been working on these kinds of problems for decades, but despite advances in behavioral modeling, virtual worlds and immersive games are still soaked in the testosterone of visual wowness. I think there are three primary reasons that avatars in virtual worlds lack emotional expression and behavioral realism:

1. Virtual world interaction evolved to a large degree within the industry of games, which emphasizes action, skill-leveling, and killer graphics over communicative expression. Socializing tools were not inherited from this ancestor medium.

2. Virtual worlds typically use a third-person view, behind the avatar, as a default vantage point, which means you are watching your avatar's derriere most of the time. Facial expressions are pointless from this vantage point. (And if you are a young male controlling Lara Croft, you may be a happy camper).

3. Many virtual world programmers are trained in math, physics, and engineering, and not in the affective sciences. Engineering culture (at least during the initial rise of virtual worlds industries) was dominant in development teams. They were also male-dominated. At the end of the day, the genetic codes to a virtual world are embedded in its software. No matter how dedicated the marketing and design teams may be in specifying social-interaction requirements, the world-view of the developers makes its way into the code, especially in strongly software engineer-oriented companies.

For these reasons, virtual world and game companies are just not set up to streamline the development of emotive avatars. According to Raph Koster, "Given the cost of doing any of this stuff beyond the minimum, the hope for better avatar body language, then, rests in the casual market, and the worldy worlds, because those are the only markets which privilege it. And even these struggle with the puppeteering, because all of these systems have interfaces that increase in complexity and likely user confusion as the capabilities increase. In the name of balancing resources and keeping the interface clean, developers lean towards less emotional bandwidth. It might be the case that World of Warcraft could significantly extend the lifetime of a customer by adding better puppeteering, but weighing the benefits against the opportunity costs of more armor sets has thus far come down in favor of less emotion and more ease of use, less communication and more monster killing" (Koster 2009).

This situation has started to change due to the rise of online social networking, and a newer generation of virtual worlds being developed for the purpose of socializing and remote collaboration. The emphasis is shifting from *things* to *people*. And from people-as-3D-rendered-things to people-as-communicating agents. It also helps that there are more female programmers joining the industry.

Juanita Marquez is the linguist ex-girlfriend of Hiro Protagonist, in Neal Stephenson's *Snow Crash*. Juanita knows that

"...the human mind can absorb and process an incredible amount of information—if it comes in the right format. The right interface. If you put the right face on it" (1992). She programmed the avatar facial expressions for the Black Sun (an exclusive hangout in the Metaverse), and this is what made it such a success. Of course Juanita is fictitious, and so is her avatar tech. But what she represents for virtual world development is real.

Geek Syndrome

Consider this evolution: text cursor → mouse cursor → Pong paddle → PacMan → Mario → Lara Croft → the modern avatar. The modern avatar has lots of genes inherited from the evolution of computer gaming. Maybe that's why it is not so good at socializing. There is ongoing research to determine whether autism has a genetic factor, and if so, how do the genetic factors interact with the environmental factors. I would like to put forth the following claim for debate: avatars have inherited the genetic codes of gaming, and because of this they suffer from a kind of *virtual autism*: a lack of social engagement, insufficient eye-contact, and repetitive animation.

I have some intimate experience with avatars—that is, their insides—what makes them tick (or not tick, as is it were). My goal has always been to de-geekify avatar design. This can only be accomplished by infusing an ethos of social literacy into low-level software. Avatar code must evolve a limbic system, a cerebellum, mirror neurons, hippocampi, and a *communication homunculus* (stay tuned for what on earth I might mean by all of this). In short, I believe that avatars must be de-geekified —from the inside out.

In matters of working out tough design problems, one place to look for inspiration is biology. You may have already detected some biological themes emerging in this book. Now let's dive right in.

3

From Microbes to Post-Humans

"Language is the source of misunderstandings."
— Antoine de Saunt-Exupéry, *The Little Prince*

Sexual attraction, fear, and other primal emotions are associated with specific pheromones in human perspiration which produce a scent that is usually not registered consciously. The terms, "I smell fear", or "we had a chemical attraction to each other" have a scientific basis. Chemicals may have been the basis for communication in microscopic organisms in the oceans of early Earth. These organisms are our ancestors.

The combination of scent, perception of bodily gesture and facial expression, and prosody of the voice—all of these simultaneous signals—create a sensorium that we process, mostly unconsciously, as we communicate. Communication is naturally multimodal, taking advantage of all available senses and physical media. On the fleshy end of the spectrum are the *somatic* senses: touch, temperature, pain, proprioception and balance. On the less-fleshy side are taste, smell, hearing, and vision. We can talk about a general hierarchy of senses. The senses involving touch are based on physical contact; balance and proprioception are related to how our own bodies are being held or moving in the world. The senses of taste and smell are based on chemistry, the sense of hearing is based on air vibration, and the sense of vision is based on light. The order of this list is roughly associated with speed: light travels faster than sound waves, and sound waves travel faster then chemical transfer. Chemical communication is generally faster than communication by touch: a moth may smell a few molecules from a potential mate, carried by the wind, before it physically arrives to mate. (On the other hand, it is possible that you might feel a slap in the face before you smell the emotion of the slapper).

There are three main sensory channels for animal communication: 1. chemical, 2. acoustical, and 3. visual. If you draw a triangle with the three vertices representing these channels, you can plot various examples of animals inside the triangle, arranged according to the degree to which they use these channels for communication. (There are other channels, such as tactile and electrical, but these are sufficiently rare so as to omit from the graph). E. O. Wilson drew such a triangle in his book, *Sociobiology*. He plotted humans right up against the edge that connects the vertices for visual and acoustical channels—far away from the chemical channel (Wilson 1975). Humans were plotted much closer to the acoustical vertex than the visual vertex, owing perhaps to the fact that humans traditionally communicate using speech. I suspect that human communication actually spreads along this edge quite a bit, and some human cultures use the visual channel more than others. Furthermore, I would suspect that our communications are becoming more visual all the time, as our interactions become increasingly mediated (consider that reading and writing are primarily visual activities).

The reason I begin this chapter with some biology is to place the subject of human body language in a wide context: within the functioning of the biosphere, which has been in operation for a very long time. Human communication is a recent blip in evolutionary time. Let's consider the various forms of body language emerging on the internet as the latest micro-blips in this long history. But before exploring the long view, I want to first give a few personal anecdotes.

Personal Note

I am sitting here in Turk's Coffee Lounge in Vancouver, BC (my "office" during this initial book-writing sabbatical). Instead of working on my laptop, I am people-watching. I have always been a people-watcher, but now I do it with conviction, dedication, and scholarly focus—complete with piercing eyes and furrowed brow (and smiles, when appropriate). My lifelong interest in body language dates back to my childhood: it was my primary mode of communication. In fact, I was so "nonverbal" that my parents worried whether I had a learning disability, or worse, some kind of brain disorder. My sister Betcey, on the other hand, was very vocal. Even though she was two years younger, she could talk circles around me. Betcey has memories of my mother carrying me in her arms as I was waking up in the morning, still rubbing my eyes. She would tell my mother, "Jeffrey is hungry". Mom would ask me what I wanted to eat. I would point towards the food cupboard, and my mother would ask me what I was pointing at. Betcey would then say, "He wants crackers and milk. He always wants crackers and milk". Betcey was my mouthpiece. In fact, she jokes that I helped her to become a better speaker!

I was a poor student throughout school, until I began studying art in college. I was never good at listening to the teacher, especially if there were no visual aids, or if the teacher was not very animated. Later in life, I realized that I had come to rely heavily on the signals that surround the string of words being delivered to me. This included intonation of voice, facial expressions, the reactions of other students, and even environmental factors. I sometimes wonder at times if I even heard people's words at all as they spoke; I had become so good at hearing the spaces between the words, and seeing, feeling, sensing the environment that gave the words context and meaning. Henry Ward Beecher wrote, "All words are pegs to hang ideas on". I remember liking this quote the first time I read it. I had always been good at coming up with ideas; it's just I could never find the pegs. Dyslexics make up for their handicap by becoming highly-tuned to nonverbal signals. Psychologist Catya von Károlyi suggests that dyslexics are naturally talented in this way, and that dyslexia could be characterized, not as a disorder, but as a special talent, featuring visual-spatial skills (Károlyi et al. 2003).

Let's take the long evolutionary view again: creating and interpreting nonverbal signals is an ancient skill that we share with most animals. But the ability to speak words, place visual symbols into long one-dimensional strings, and parse sentences, emerged quite recently, in the grand scheme of things.

You Can't Turn it Off

Your body language cannot be turned off. Witness this while looking at a person having an engaging phone conversation. At times there can be much excited waving of the hands. And in a crowded shopping area, someone can get accidentally smacked in the face if they aren't watching.

I once noticed a fellow standing on a street corner with a cell phone. I watched as he uttered a long, drawn-out word, and with it, a magnificent arch of the spine, even bending his knees. If I could perform it for you I would, and you would recognize the expression immediately, even though there is no name for this expression.

I remember walking down a quiet side street one evening in the 1980s. I thought I heard the sound of a conversation up ahead of me, but when I looked, there was only one person. I wondered if he was speaking on a cell phone, but both of his arms were free and he occasionally waved his hands around, shrugging, pointing, etc. At the time, there were not as many cell phone users as there are now, and there were certainly not as many users of hands-free headsets. I concluded (correctly) that he was using a headset. I had caught a glimpse of the future on that day.

When I study people talking on the phone, I think about how many calories are being burned while making these motions—motions that are never seen by the person at the other end of the line. From the standpoint of energy efficiency, this seems quite wasteful. It doesn't fit the Darwinian fitness equation. Why would a person expend so much unused energy? The answer is that telephones are artificial mediators of human communication, and they were invented only recently in evolutionary time, whereas our innate physical communication instincts evolved over several millions of years—many of which were already in place before we became human.

From Gesture to Speech

There are several theories on the origin of language, and we may never come to an exact answer regarding how or when it evolved. One theory, called *Gestural Theory*, claims that human speech emerged from the primal energy of gestures (Hewes 1973). Brain studies show that neural structures for gesture are similar to those of vocal speech, and they occur right next to each other in the brain.

There are several possible explanations for why a shift may have occurred from a primarily gestural form of communication to predominately vocal form. According to one explanation, the hands of Homo Sapiens started being used more for tool manipulation, and so they were less available for gesturing: vocal sounds had to step in and take their place. Otherwise, a tool-user in the middle of an important task would have to drop everything just to respond to a question like, "Did you remember to take out the trash?" Another explanation is that vocal sounds can be heard without the receiver having to look at the sender, thus allowing communication in darkness or with visual obstacles.

Primates use gesturing and visual signaling (left: chimp sketches by Ventrella; right: orangutan: http://www.pdclipart.org/)

It is likely that there are multiple factors that converged at a certain time in our evolution, creating a ripe environment for speech to evolve. Communicative gesture is likely to have been one factor. Gestural Theory helps to explain why body language is nearly impossible to turn off, especially when we are talking. Jana Iverson, a researcher who studies the connections between gesture and speech, says that gesturing, thinking, and speaking are tightly woven. Scientific experiments demonstrate that individuals who are blind from birth will gesture when they talk, even though they have never learned to gesture from watching others (Iverson et al. 2000).

Okay, I have probably gone on enough about something which is obvious: we humans gesture, and we do it a lot, especially when we are talking. Now the question is: how conscious have we become of our gesturing? Can gesturing be elevated to an art?

The Art of Body Language

We often hear that "your body doesn't know how to lie", as suggested in the 1971 book *Body Language*, by Julius Fast (1971). Oft-sited examples of how to read other people's body language include looking for crossed legs and crossed arms as indication of a "closed" attitude— an example that many people have since tossed into the cliché bucket. These basic indicators of an observed person's mood and intent may be good rules-of-thumb, but I believe that these indicators do not capture the true subtlety and utility of body language and the role it plays in human society. Geoffrey Beattie, author of *Visible Thought*, says that psychologists traditionally overemphasized body language as an emotional non-verbal side-effect (Beattie 2003). Body language is a lot more than some unconscious phenomenon observed in others, like animals being studied in a laboratory. It is an art, perfected over eons by storytellers and actors. My friend Alan Sperling is a character animator. When I first met Alan I asked him what he did for a living. He told me that he is an actor. It just happens that he acts through his characters. Actors and character animators generate body language all the time—it's all in a days work. There is nothing invisible or unconscious about their craft.

Body language has not only become more conscious and deliberate in this increasingly visual culture, but it is about to take on an even more conscious role in our lives within the subcultures of virtual worlds. Why? Because this stuff doesn't come *naturally* to avatars. Okay, *nothing* comes *naturally* to avatars. The point is that the difficulty of doing online body language necessitates conscious effort. This may change if the technology for avatar puppetry becomes so intuitive that its users forget that the tools are even there—like the way designers and scientists sketching ideas on paper rarely think about the fact that they are holding pencils in their hands. Unless or until this technology becomes so transparent, virtual body language will continue to require conscious effort.

Authenticity

Umberto Eco, in *A Theory of Semiotics*, explores the notion of lying with one's body. Gesturing can have signification to an interpreter, even if the gesturing is not consciously intended as communication. However it is not easy (and maybe not possible) to know if a gesturer is *not* conscious of his own body language. For instance, a gesturer may pretend to be gesturing unconsciously (such as feigning the characteristic movements of particular culture with the purpose of trying to form a bond with the other person). The interpreter likewise may be aware of this "lie", and pretend not to notice ("lying to the lie").

This recursive game of pretend can get quite convoluted. But in fact it happens all the time between people. This raises a question for me concerning avatar users who are aware of their puppeteering actions. Even if those actions come out looking "natural", are they not lies? I think the answer depends on how much of your true self is being projected onto your avatar. A user who is wired to the hilt with motion capture gear driving a fully-articulated avatar may not be able to hold back all the unconscious movements that reveal emotion. This user would be a valid target for *Ekman-like* scrutiny (Paul Ekman is the famed psychologist whose research the basis for the television series, *Lie To Me*). In this case, many of the same principles would apply to the avatar as they would with in-the-flesh bodily lying and truth-telling. But when considering the more constrained, more common everyday mediated interfaces for puppeteering avatar expression, the question of body language authenticity gets fuzzy. Your true self may not shine through. This could have consequences for business, education, and diplomacy.

Jonathan Gratch of USC and colleagues have done experiments with virtual agents that generate *rapport*. These experiments involve social signaling, responsive feedback, and behavioral mimicry. In one experiment, Gratch reports that subjects found a "virtual rapport agent" to be more engaging than a real human (Gratch et al. 2007). If you put enough time, effort and ingenuity into making a virtual human respond favorably, politely, and positively to a human, you can make that human feel good about him or herself, and the virtual agent as well.

Rapport can be genuine—emerging from sincere interactions between people, either face-to-face, or through avatars (although with considerably more effort). Alternatively it can be fabricated though a high-tech form of virtual lying. I could despise every cell in your body, but if I'm using a *Rapport Agent* to converse with you, you might never know it. Indeed something like this happens all the time in our professional lives as we cover up our less attractive, less productive emotions in order to engage in polite and respectful behavior. But there may be a fundamental difference when it comes to virtual worlds. Judith Donath of the MIT Media Lab considers the consequences of virtual rapport. She refers to one of the experiments by Jeremy Bailenson demonstrating that avatars programmed to mimic a subject's gestures were more well-liked and persuasive. Donath claims that this is fundamentally different than what happens in the real world: "I would argue that the automatic simulation of mimicry is fundamentally different, even from the most deliberate and calculated of face to face imitations. The candidate who copies the clothes and cadences of his or her potential voters, or the empathy-faking listener, must at least pay close attention to the actions of their audience and experience acting like them. When the mimicry is transposed to the virtual world, the person behind the avatar experiences no such affinity. The intimacy is purely illusory" (Donath 2010).

Consider the ways in which we will use avatars, not just to socialize, express, and create, but to persuade, win friends, and influence people. For this reason, I would suggest that *authenticity* be considered an important differentiator when comparing and contrasting social virtual worlds and collaborative environments. When the virtual world is dedicated to creativity and role playing, like

Second Life or World of Warcraft, authenticity and transparency are not so critical. If I pop over to a Democratic Party World, or an Adult Furry World, or a Pentecostal Church World, then I expect some overarching ideology to permeate the matrix. I would expect this to affect the way my avatar behaves. If I jump into a virtual Disney World, for instance, my beard would be instantly shaved off and my avatar would have a smile so wide that my head would be nearly split in half. I would not have the ability to make lewd sexual gestures to passersby.

Here's a different scenario: If I need to gather around a virtual table with grandma, mom, and the family doctor in order to discuss grandpa's declining health and to go over photographs to include in a memorial web site, I don't want any corporate, political, or religious ideologies changing the way I look and act. This is a family affair, and we need to be in total control of our expressions. One may well argue that this kind of situation calls for a video conference, where there is less risk of having our sincere communications mediated by opaque communication technology.

Lying and truth-telling, and all the gradations and colorings in-between are a part of our normal communicative life. The air and light that exists between you and me as we use natural language is *neutral*. The same cannot always be said for the technologies that mediate our virtual interactions.

And yet, might it still be possible for a virtual world to become a reliable conductor of truth and authenticity? When this communication medium matures more and becomes more plastic, it may allow for the whole range of human expression (or, more likely, new kinds of expressions—*messages of the medium*). Emergent nonverbal and verbal language, visual symbols established by social contract, and sufficiently-rich user-generated content may eventually provide enough authenticity signals for genuine human interaction.

I can only hope that there will always remain the means for me to create a genuine nonverbal lie on the internet—*my* lie, and no one else's.

Why The Frown? You Look Much Better When it's Upside-Down

When we use the term "software user interface", we are often referring to the pixel-based rectangle of light coming from a computer screen. Our ability to apprehend this as a surface in which to give and receive information was primed over the last several million years, as the human face evolved to become flatter and as the features of the eyes and mouth clarified visually. The face is a proto-image. It has evolved in shape, color, and texture from a fuzzy, longish, nose and ear-dominated object to a more flat, eye and mouth-dominated sign. Two faces facing each other become user interfaces that are getting and giving signals. The human face might be regarded as the original user interface of Homo Sapiens. Standard books are approximately the size of a human head, as are many e-books and the Apple iPad. It's an ancient ergonomic form factor.

Even as the human embryo develops from a fishy wisp, growing gills and other vestiges of ancestral evolution (and then deleting them, as if to say, "Been there, done that, ready to Go Human"), the face starts preparing for a life of human interfacing. The eyes and nostrils, which start widely separated, migrate to the front of the head, and the embryo starts blinking, sticking out its tongue, smiling and frowning. It's rehearsing.

Image: Joanna Robinson

What's the difference between a smile and a frown? If you ask a 4-year-old in the midst of drawing a picture of a happy Mommy and Daddy, and her older sister who is sad because she fell off her bike, the answer might be that a frown is an upside-down smile. This could be confirmed by a parent or an art teacher turning the drawing upside-down. A sweet little 4-year-old theory emerges. Should the art teacher discredit this theory and instead explain the nature of human emotion and the physiology of facial muscles? The child's first principles of facial signaling might be perfectly valid: mental scaffolding that can be later used to ratchet up to a more accurate understanding of the human face and expression.

Several facial animation systems have been developed that model expressions on a detailed physical level of simulation, taking into account the actual muscles involved. Some of these systems are proposed as having applications for social virtual worlds. The developers of these systems are missing the point. According to Daniel McNeill, author of *The Face* (1998), "We seem to view not muscle movements, but the shifts and surges of the mind itself". For social virtual worlds, a language of facial communication must be abstracted away from the details of musculature. It should correspond with the cognitive and social mechanisms that emerge above and beyond the physiology of muscle and bone.

With a cartoon face, a smile could in fact be characterized as an upside-down frown, as the child art student has proclaimed. For realistic faces however, more parameters are required to simulate a smile. Consider that an authentic smile, sometimes called the "Duchenne smile", involves more than just stretching the sides of the mouth outward and upward. The orbicularis oculi muscles are involved, raising the cheeks and changing the shape of the eyes, making them more crescent-shaped; here is another visual descriptor to use in a facial expression language. In fact, there is a special way that a face can be made to sparkle which involves only the *smiling eyes* of the

Duchenne smile, but *not* the smiling mouth.

Oops: you may have noticed that I used the word "muscle"—right after proclaiming that the language of facial expression is not about muscles. You might argue that I cannot get around the fact that muscles are the foundation of facial expressions. Of course they are involved in the machinery. But for our purposes, the messages that get passed from one eye-brain system to another are not about muscles; these messages are part of an ancient visual language which functions on a higher level than the visceral machinery of faces.

There.com avatar expressions (Image: Francis 7)

Prosthetic Avatar Cars

In taking a long evolutionary view, how shall we characterize body language as manifested in current technology? Is there a consistent thread that extends from the remote past to the distant future? Our bodies are increasingly extending beyond our animal selves into our photographs, our cars, and our Facebook pages. Marshall McLuhan proclaimed that our nervous systems now extend beyond our individual bodies (*outering*). Artist and virtual world philosopher Mark Stephen Meadows says, "Car is Avatar is Prosthetic" (2008). The car, as a means of transportation, has become a prosthesis for human locomotion. The avatar, as embodiment in virtual worlds, becomes a prosthesis for identity and expression. Let's broaden our definition of "body language" now, extending the notion of *body* to be anything that can be seen, and which *stands for* a communicator. Let's start with a primitive element of modern visual communication: type fonts.

Edward Tufte points out that pictorial information had existed in written text in the time of Leonardo who inserted small graphical drawings along with his text in his manuscripts (1990). Galileo added tiny outlines of the shape of Saturn in-line with the rest of the type in a text he wrote in 1613. These symbols were probably carved in woodblocks or lead, and inserted directly into the book press (Tufte 2006). Tufte himself has followed in this tradition in his books with crafty intermingling of words, typography, and pictures. (Awesome— ☺ I just discovered a bunch of symbols ♥ here ☛ in my word processing software :-) Written text has been on a continual path of increasing visualness. There was very little punctuation in the early days following the invention of the printing press. Over time, more punctuation, formatting, and typographical styles have emerged.

Eyebrow: Distant Ancestor to the Circumflex Accent

As we weave this evolutionary narrative, let's imagine the accents used in typography, such as the circumflex (û), the umlaut (ë) and the tilde (ñ), as *eyebrows*, dancing along the tops of words as our reading eyes skim across them.

Now let's imagine emoticons as forms of punctuation that are the primordial ancestors of modern avatars. The elements of the human face have crept into text, mostly indirectly but in some cases directly. Most obvious is the *smiley*. Ancestors to modern smileys have existed in varied forms. Combinations of type fonts or punctuation were used to create simple pictograms for nonverbal expression. As far back as the 1800s, the Morse code symbol 88 was used for "hugs and kisses". The symbol -) was once proposed as a way to indicate a joke (indicating "tongue in cheek"). Writers such as Vladimir Nabokov and Ambrose Bierce had expressed a desire for punctuation to indicate smiles. In 2001, Scott Fahlman, a computer scientist at CMU, proposed to his colleagues that they use the symbols... :-)   :-(... while using internet chat to indicate when they were joking around, so as not to offend someone expecting serious business. Lynne Truss, author of *Eats, Shoot & Leaves*, calls the emoticon "...the greatest (or most desperate, depending on how you look at it) advance in punctuation since the question mark in the reign of Charlemagne" (2003).

Punctuation Made from Punctuation

;
-   ⟶ ;-)
)

The smiley is an organism that evolved out of smaller, simpler punctuation marks. Any time we use old symbols to construct new symbols, we build more communication scaffolding. It's like biology. According to Endosymbiotic theory, the organelles inside of eukaryotic cells (the kind of cells that we're made of) were once simple individual organisms themselves (prokaryotes) who took up residence in each others' bodies; that's about as intimate as a symbiotic relationship can get! This concept was championed and articulated by biologist Lynn Margulis. So, that means the *smiley* is a *Margulian* entity, a *eukaryotic* organism. Like other language entities, it has ascended the scaffolding, building new symbols out of existing symbols.

The internet enables us to communicate with people on the other side of the world on a regular basis. This immediacy of communication comes with the expectations of nuance that face-to-face communication affords. That is why inserting body language into text is so important now. The time spans between writing and reading have shortened. The written word is becoming a medium of real-time conversation—a rather strange and unlikely occupation for something that was invented for a much more premeditated usage.

Gajadhar and Green (2005) did a study with a group of students who used online chat for discussions and collaborations in a college course. The lecturer introduced nonverbal elements early on in the discussions which were then mirrored by the students as the discussion continued. Spontaneous uses of onomatopoeia, exclamation points, and other nonverbal elements were used. It was found that many of these elements were used to build rapport and establish connectedness. The researchers found that the students were very creative in the way they appropriated old typographical symbols and applied them in new ways. *Exaptation* is a term suggested by Gould and Vrba to explain the way in which some trait in an organism is co-opted for a new and different purpose (1982). The strange fact of realtime conversations using typographic forms is creating reappropriation of typography to create body language.

Several punctuation symbols have been proposed for getting subtle messages across, such as the *irony mark*: "؟" The need to be clear about irony or sarcastic innuendo has become so dire that a company was formed specifically to invent a new emoticon called the "sarcmark". Lord knows we've all had that horrible experience of trying to be funny in an email message and the recipient took it the wrong way, causing much wringing of hands and several follow-up emails to clear up the confusion. Here is a bit of advertising found on sarcmark.com: "…

Never again be misunderstood! Never again waste a good sarcastic line on someone who doesn't get it! Sarcasm - Punctuate It - SarcMark ®. Stand Up For Sarcasm - It needs a punctuation mark. Let your voice and written word be heard across the country, the continent, and the world" (Sarcmark.com).

www.sarcmark.com

The menagerie of new typographic species emerging to overcome misunderstanding has become a viable economic force. Today, the smiley is so common that our word-processing and email applications parse commonly used smileys and replace them with little circular smiley faces. Perhaps the sarcmark will acquire a face some day.

I often use the smiley *in place of* a period, because it serves a similar purpose for me; it lends closure to a string of text. It's like a *friendly* period. I also like to use it as the right-hand side of a parenthetical statement (for those friendly-type side comments :)

Now allow me to rant for just a moment. I have become a satisfied user of the smiley and the frowny, and a few other emoticons, for all the usual reasons. But when I type a smiley into a Microsoft Word document, my :) is hijacked and replaced with a graphical icon of a smiley face. In some text applications, the hijacker smiley even comes with a silly animation. Each application has its own visual style. The temptation of the software developers to add this feature is understandable; it is a cute trick. But it robs me of my choice of body language representation. To me, it is better to have the dry, typographical symbol that is consistent with the type font that I am using, than to have a cute animation appear in my text without my permission.

Smileys: (left: Ventrella; right: http://www.pdclipart.org/)

An Alien has Invaded my Text!

My visceral reaction to the hijacking of my smiley punctuation by cute yellow faces is not unlike my reaction to the Microsoft Office Assist paper clip (Clippy) and the Windows Search Dog, both of which I would happily delete using a virtual bazooka, were that provided as part of the user interface. Catherine, whom we met at the beginning of this book, gripes that her :P in chat applications gets converted into an icon of a goofy, drunken smile. She uses :P for different purposes, and would rather it remain in the typographic universe so that its affect can be based on context, not pictorial style. She does not want it to color her meaning in any way external to the mere fact that she is using it. Catherine and I are both of the camp that believes that the smiley should remain a typographical species, and not be converted automatically into a pictorial icon whose personality and emotional effect are determined by an icon artist who doesn't know me. In essence, we believe emoticons are a form of punctuation, and they should not be hijacked into the pictorial realm, any more than the word "leaf" should be converted into a picture of a leaf. Granted, some people like to add cool-looking smileys into their text, because they can't generate it with typographical symbols. In this case, the smiley (or *leaf*, or whatever) can be considered as a tiny illustration embedded into the text, like the graphical symbols inserted by Leonardo, Galileo, and Tufte.

What's the real point of my rant about pictorial smileys hijacking my text? It all comes back to the question of me being the owner of my body language—a theme that will be threading its way back into this book several times. Now it is time to bring the topic of punctuation back to the realm of avatars.

Punctuation as Expression Hyperlinks

Here's another interesting evolutionary branch: the use of textual punctuation to trigger an avatar's visual expressions (if there is an avatar involved). In some online games and virtual worlds, when an emoticon is typed into the user's chat window, it causes the avatar to play an associated gesture or facial expression. The symbol "/" followed by an action word is often used to make an avatar perform that action. For instance, the text, "It's nice to see you again. /smile How have you been?" causes the avatar to smile after the chat string has been issued. The "/smile" text may or may not be distributed as part of the chat that others can see, depending on the virtual world or game being used. Various online games and virtual worlds parse commonly used texts such, as LOL, and automatically make the avatar do that action.

Here we see an example of punctuation (or some text-based string) that is not converted into a pictorial representation within the text itself, but is used to animate a pictorial representation outside of the text—a hyperlink of sorts. Assuming one is chatting with an avatar on hand to play expressions as he/she is typing away, could the avatar then perform all punctuation for the user, as if the text were rigged with puppet strings? What would happen if this idea were taken to the extreme? I can imagine that a fully-rigged text might appear as if some kind of choreographer's notation had invaded it, turning it into a frightening Rube Goldbergian tangle. But, like the innards of WYSIWYG web design tools, it may be ugly on the inside, but what it does on the outside can be expressive, elegant and meaningful. Since reading and writing are marching toward each other to occupy the realm of real-time conversation, there is more need to include the nonverbal element. So, we might yet see a whole menagerie of punctuations emerging...with puppet strings attached, poised and ready for an avatar to animate.

That Mouse Cursor is *Me*

I remember recording a videotape explaining a software interface that I had designed. While I was recording the computer screen and my voice to explain the different parts of the interface, I found myself moving the mouse cursor around as an annotative pointing device. I didn't think it would actually show up in the final video. It was just automatic—something that I compulsively do when exploring an interface or explaining code to a fellow engineer. While a mouse cursor might get in the way of some screen-captured videos, in this case, it turned out to be useful, in retrospect. The cursor became "me", and its motions reflected what I was saying and what I was referring to on the screen. My mouse cursor became a very simple avatar—a tiny Vanna White ⤢ helping to direct the viewer's attention.

While browsing the web, if I place my mouse cursor over a hyperlink to another web page, I am moving myself to the location of a portal. If I click, then I teleport to a new web page. The mouse cursor becomes a constant in the otherwise fragmented, dimensionless space of the internet. With webcasting software, one's mouse cursor becomes a simple expressive entity that is perceived by others in remote locations; it becomes a distributed agent. And for collaboration tools that allow multiple mouse cursors to be broadcast and seen by all participants, now we're looking at something that could be described as a primitive avatar system. Multi-cursor desktop sharing tools represent a break from the single-user, single-focus realm of the lonely desktop. It also allows several remote people to come together as *avatars*—simple avatars!—and to generate just a tiny bit of social body language. Michael Heim, author of *The Metaphysics of Virtual Reality*, wrote the following about cursors and avatars in an online piece entitled "The Avatar and the Power Grid":

"The avatar first arises in the most primitive form as a moving cursor on the grid screen when that screen becomes networked with other screens. The cursor on the user's screen opens a mouse hole in the unified power grid. Through the moving cursor we see revealed the mind of a human subject who is navigating information. The appearance of a tiny cursor movement in networked environments - as the cursor movement becomes visible on all client computers on the network - causes a unique flicker in the power grid of computer systems that control vast amounts of information. The mouse moves, the cursor crosses the screen, and with that movement the human subject, who would otherwise be concealed by the screens, stands forth. Though tiny in relation to the larger terrain of the computer screen, the cursor points to a mouse that roars. The mouse bespeaks an alternate notion of computer space where the information grid is shot through with human subjectivity. The cursor mouse becomes the seed of the avatar, the potential of cyberspace to mix information with intersubjectivity and with real-time communication" (Heim 2001).

Virtual Embodiment

All these various nonverbal entities I've just discussed can be seen as primitive forms of *embodiment*: type fonts, punctuation marks, smileys, mouse cursors. The notion of virtual embodiment is a busy meme. This is partly due to the increased ubiquity and ambience of computing, the birth of the world wide web, and the emergence of virtual worlds. Some would argue that it is inevitable: since software is prosthetic to human cognition, it follows that we should enter into the digital worlds that we create in the same way that we have always entered into our what-if scenarios and our narratives. The internet is a dynamic, interactive, cognitive ecosystem. A language of embodiment *must naturally* emerge within it.

I have just taken you through a brief tour of several related subjects: the origins of body language and speech, truth-telling and lying on the internet, how technology mediates our expression, and how the written word—and interfaces in general—have become populated with various forms of virtual body language. The avatar can be seen as an extension of this evolution of technologically-mediated body language. Seeing the phenomenon of the avatar through this wide-angle lens may help us to apply smart design principles to the creation of social virtual worlds, and to software interfaces in general. In the next chapter I will give a real-world account of the creation of an avatar system which takes into account many of these biological first principles.

4

Avatar-Centric Communication

In the summer of 1997, Will Harvey sent me a fax from Switzerland describing a vision he had for a virtual world. He was on a ski trip, and that day he had been riding on a ski-lift, and chatting with a charming young woman. The whole sensorium—the magnificent view, the fun, bouncy mechanics of the ski-lift, and of course, the charming companion—left an impression in Will's mind. Will is a game developer and computer scientist who had his first success at a young age and went on to become a Silicon Valley entrepreneur. In 1995 Will hired me to work at Rocket Science Games in San Francisco. The dot com bubble was quivering, and two years later Rocket Science went out of business. That's when Will had his vision on the slopes, and that's when he asked me to join him in prototyping a virtual world that was later named "There". In the following years, Will and I were to have many creative coding sessions and illuminating conversations about avatars, virtual worlds physics, and emergent gameplay.

I recall sitting down to write the very first line of code for the prototype. My first goal was to get something to show up on the screen that represented the user. "Start simple", I thought. "This is going to be a long evolution". I started by whipping together a 3D environment—the proverbial flat horizontal grid against a black background—a rather cliché image, symbolizing the sleek geometrical perfection of cyberspace. I had always considered those vast flat grids extending out into infinity as symbolizing the *loneliness* of virtual reality. In the back of my mind, I had a feeling that this lonely grid would be temporary.

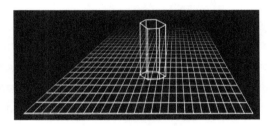

My first avatar (Image: Ventrella)

To represent the user, I created an upright wireframe cylinder standing on the horizontal grid (it was so crude that it had only six sides!) I set the point of view (the virtual camera) in this 3D world at a location next to the cylinder, slightly raised and aimed slightly downward—your basic third-person view. You may ask: how much is there to say about moving a cylinder around on a flat plane? Actually, representing a user as a cylinder on a horizontal surface comes with a load of design considerations. For instance, how fat? How tall? How should the user tell the cylinder to move forward, or turn? If it is controlled with the mouse, what mouse motions should control moving forward versus turning around? And how fast should these motions occur as a function of mouse movement? Can the cylinder tilt on its vertical axis? Should the viewpoint stay fixed in space or should it follow the cylinder? If so, how closely? These were fundamental questions that played an important role in making the cylinder "feel like me". I wanted it to be easy and natural to move around in the world. These fundamental first principles of navigation, it turns out, remained just as important as the avatar evolved into a human form in the years that followed.

Primitive Beginnings

Let's drill down into this a bit more. Why might one start with a cylinder as opposed to some other simple shape, such as a sphere or a cube? Think about the human body for a moment. We are bipedal mammals who occupy a mostly vertical volume when we stand or walk. A vertical volume...with the possible exception of people who consume sufficient numbers of McDonald's hamburgers so as to approach spherehood. Human eyes and brains understand the world most easily with a roughly horizontal line of sight, head upright. The three semicircular canals of each inner ear are oriented approximately orthogonal to each other, and each corresponds to one of three axes of head rotation. The lateral (horizontal) canal actually becomes perpendicular to gravity and parallel to the ground when the head is pitched down 30 degrees as if to be looking at the ground a few meters in front of the feet while walking or running. Just another one of the many reminders that humans are walking machines.

A vertically-oriented navigation system comes naturally to bipedal mammals. A cylinder represents this verticality, as well as having rotational affordance, which is manifest in the roundness about the vertical axis.

The Social Life of a Cylinder

I'm not ready to come back to the slopes of the Matterhorn and the charming ski-lift companion just yet. First I want to do a thought-experiment to examine the limits and possibilities of avatar body language. For this thought experiment I want to greatly reduce the degrees of freedom of the avatar in order to point out the many ways of generating body language, even with a limited vocabulary of movement. This is to help prepare us to explore the entire realm of body language, and it will also provide the context for reviewing a bit of avatar history.

Consider a virtual world with text chat as in a typical instant-messaging application. The avatars are cylinders, which have "noses" (or some feature that serves to indicate where the front side of the avatar is as it rotates).

Locomotion affordance in sphere, cylinder, and cylinder with "nose" (Image: Ventrella)

You can move these cylinders around on a horizontal surface and turn them in place - as if they were being rolled around on coasters. Given this constraint on avatar movement, what kinds of body language can we possibly create? At first you might think, "None! How can you have body language if you have no moving parts?" But in fact, there is quite a bit of fundamental body language that you could create, such as:

1. moving up to another avatar and facing it while you are chatting with it
2. NOT facing the avatar while you are chatting with it (to express aloofness, shyness, indirection, discreetness, etc.)
3. standing next to the avatar you are chatting with but facing in the same direction as the other avatar, as if you were both

watching the same scene (a behavior that is seen in men more than in women)

4. turning completely in the opposite direction from the avatar you are chatting with and deliberately facing away

5. standing in place and rotating (perhaps to express that you are completely out of your mind)

6. revolving around another avatar (to annoy, get attention, or make that avatar feel trapped)

7. repeatedly moving towards and away from the avatar you are chatting with

8. standing abnormally far away from the avatar you are chatting with, or conversely, standing extremely close

9. occasionally turning and facing a third avatar that you are talking about as a form of referencing

10. standing and watching a distant avatar which is moving along, and continually adjusting your rotation so you are always facing that avatar, as if to be watching it

As you can see, not having an articulated body doesn't mean that you can't have nonverbal communication. In fact, we could probably come up with more examples than the ones listed. Furthermore, arbitrary behaviors can easily take on new meaning above and beyond the natural signals that animals create with bodily proximity, relative motion, direction, etc. And so the possibilities are essentially endless.

I have just described a fundamental base level vocabulary of body language that can be used no matter what kind of avatar you have (as long as it has a horizontal heading and as long as you can move it and rotate it around its vertical axis). A lot of this stuff falls within the realm of *Proxemics*: the study of measurable distances between people and the associated interactions and effects. The birth of shared virtual worlds has added a whole new dimension—and experimental playing field—to the study of proxemics. Some virtual world researchers have observed a sensitivity to personal space—the degree of comfort that users feel based on proximity to other avatars, and how close an avatar has to be in order to make a user uneasy. Gender and culture have been found to be factors in a phenomenon called "invasion anxiety" (Nassiri et al. 2008).

Back in 1995 one of the only online virtual worlds being publicly used was Worlds Chat. Spontaneous forms of body language were invented by its dial-up users. There were no articulated gestures; avatars were like chess pieces. As Bruce Damer reminisces, "My first 'in-world' experience was ever so timidly moving up to another group of avatars in the corner of the hub just after teleporting in. I kept back from them and typed a few words to engage in conversation. I had no idea what the rules of body contact were or whether I would be rude to interject my virtual body in between conversants. Others had no idea either so this was an interesting circumstance. Soon people (probably younger than me) were whizzing around, passing right through others' avatars (there was no collision active). So the social conventions were established for body language: i.e., it was OK to move through other people but not pausing your avatar right up front of someone's view (all perspective was first person so this would occlude someone's view completely)" (Damer 2010). Right from the start, as Damer points out, users were working out conventions of body language, basically figuring it out as they went along.

Not surprisingly, *gross-motor* body language was used widely in these early worlds. In Onlive Traveler (now Digital Space Traveler), a virtual world that included voice chat, avatars were originally represented as floating heads, and users communicated using real-time voice. The audio signal of the collection of users' voices was received in stereo, and the positioning of avatars in conversation groups affected both the visual and the aural experience. Users could move these heads forward and back using the up and down arrow keys on the keyboard, and turn left and right using the left and right arrow keys. They could also pitch up and down using page-up and page-down keys. Several forms of body language emerged spontaneously in the community, including coming together in chat circles, standing close or far apart, expressing yes and no (by alternating page-up/page-down, and left/right keys), and even turning the head completely upside down to say "my user is away".

Floating avatar heads in Onlive Traveler (Image: Steve DiPaola)

Inner Ear Disease and Avatar Motion

As mentioned earlier, the three semicircular canals in the inner ear correspond to the three rotational axes commonly used in computer graphics and engineering (x, y, z—often referred to as *yaw, pitch,* and *roll*). Each canal is sensitive to a specific axis of rotation in the head. The fluid in these canals gets swished around in complicated ways, and the tiny hairs sense the flow of the fluid. The system works pretty much all the time, and so it is usually invisible to us, thanks to the tight integration of our vestibular systems with our eyes and our motor systems. We humans are accustomed to turning our heads left and right (shaking the head *no*), and pitching the head up and down (nodding *yes*). The vestibular system is well-equipped to process these two rotations. These are salient head rotations—nearly universal in human expression of the binary opposites. These rotations are a bit more universal than waggling the top of the head side-to-side like an inverted pendulum—used widely in Indian culture to express something like "sure...okay". If you are Indian, you may argue that all three rotations are equally important for body language.

One morning, after a night of too much drinking, and a wicked, week-long sinus infection, I turned around in my bed and felt something strange. I woke up to find that the light fixture hanging from the ceiling was jumping to the left wall, sweeping across the ceiling to the right wall, and then repeating, again, and again, and again. I watched in terror until the motion subsided. The repetitive sweeping was caused by nystagmus (eye-beating), an involuntary behavior triggered by signals from the inner ear—the same thing that causes dizziness after spinning in place. What I had was BPPV, a benign (and fortunately for me, temporary) inner-ear malfunction. It is caused by tiny crystals (otoconia) getting dislodged, which then slosh around against the hairs of the semicircular canals. The cure came in the form of an amazingly low-tech procedure called the Epley maneuver, which basically turns your head into a Rubik's Cube (specific changes in head orientation, done in just the right order, cause the otoconia to settle back into their usual home in the labyrinth). The doctor who performed the maneuver instructed me to avoid nodding "yes" for a week after the maneuver, as this would disturb the otoconia. This can be a difficult chore for someone who strives to be a positive person.

I learned quite a lot about the vestibular system from this experience. I didn't realize it at the time, but this experience had an effect on the way I coded avatar motions. The next stage of evolution from the cylinder-avatar was what Will and I affectionately called "Ice

Cream Cone Man", initially inspired by some of the characters that Will had developed for a game years before. Ice Cream Cone Man had a pointy bottom, and a wider top; he was an inverted cone. And on top of the cone was a sphere: the head. The pointy bottom represented a new degree of freedom—the avatar could tilt away from its vertical axis. We had a special interest in this degree of freedom because we wanted to be able to move fast in the world and to "lean-in" to our turns, lurching and banking. And my own personal inner ear experience made me acutely aware of the fact that throughout our lives, our bodies and heads are constantly moving, turning and tilting, and we manage to not fall down constantly. For me, Ice Cream Cone Man's new degree of freedom represented an important part of bodily experience.

I gave Ice Cream Cone Man an angular spring force that caused it to pop back upright if it was tilted over. A familiar meme comes to mind for a popular children's toy: "Weebles wobble but they don't fall down". To increase wobbliness, I could adjust this force to be weak (making it act drunk—slow to correct itself), or I could adjust it to be strong (upright and uptight). Tuning this force to be somewhere in-between made it *just right*. After adding a few of these degrees of freedom, and adjusting the forces, things started to get a lot more physical and fun for our dear little avatar.

Will brought in a Nintendo 64 game console, and we studied the user navigation and 3D camera behavior for Super Mario 64 (this game was very influential in our thinking, as well as for many 3D game developers at the time). Our goal in building an avatar was to make it easy and fun to zoom around in a make-believe world (like Super Mario).

Super Mario 64 (Image: Nintendo)

Ice Cream Cone Man experienced another spike in evolutionary history—rudimentary Newtonian Physics. I turned the cone into a torso-sized ovoid and raised it above the grid plane, as if it had compressible legs beneath, pushing it up so it would stay at the level of the pelvis. It still moved forward, turned left and right, and tilted. But now, when walking or running, it had a subtle up-down bobbing motion, roughly corresponding to gait. I also added more degrees of physical simulation to the avatar's body. It now had a full 3D position and a velocity, and responded to frictions and gravity. Moving forward now meant applying a linear force in the avatar's forward direction. Turning left and right meant applying an angular force around the avatar's local up axis (with a bit of Ice Cream Cone Man sideways tilt—if moving forward, just for fun).

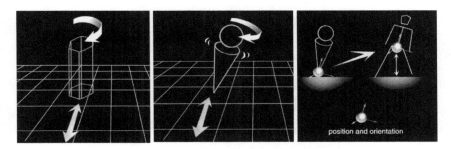

Primitive avatar locomotion acquires more degrees of freedom (Image: Ventrella)

The bobbing motions on the torso were to create the effect *as if there were walking legs underneath*, and the motions were timed to an imaginary gait. Rather than try to simulate the actual physics of legs walking (which is extremely complex), I animated simple walking legs using a technique called *inverse*  *kinematics*: a method for adjusting joint angles (like knees) so that specific endpoints (like feet) move to specific locations (like the ground). The feet stayed roughly underneath the body, and took steps when the avatar moved horizontally, and the hips stayed attached to the torso, and, most importantly, because of inverse-kinematics, the knees bent just right so as to keep everything else looking natural. The tall, gangly Abraham Lincoln was once asked, "How long are your legs?" His answer: "Long enough to reach the ground". This is how the legs worked for the avatar. They weren't part of the physical simulation—they were merely animated geometry. The reason for this abstraction was to stay focused on the overall sensation and goals of moving around in the world—which usually doesn't include minutia of legged ambulation. We wanted to keep our simulation goal-oriented. This idea will be revisited later in the chapter, "Seven Hundred Puppet Strings".

Moving Ahead

I gave the head special treatment, as far as body parts go. One technique I used (which is also used in other avatar systems) causes the head to turn *before* the body turns. I used a simple physics algorithm for this: when the user rotates the avatar, it doesn't immediately start turning. The avatar has a bit of *rotational*

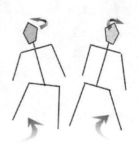

inertia, and so it ramps up its rotation within the first fraction of a second when the user starts rotating, and after the user stops rotating, it ramps-down for a fraction of a second. (The same applies for the avatar's position in space: *translational inertia*). These effects come for free when a physics model is used, and the effects of friction and mass can be delicately tweaked to make avatar navigation intuitive and satisfying (again, inspired by Mario).

Now consider that the head is much lighter than the body, and that it is also where the brain and eyes are. So it makes sense to give the head a bit less simulated mass (or none at all), so it can turn more quickly and responsively when the user changes rotation via the mouse or keyboard. The net effect is that the avatar seems to "anticipate" the turns. This was but one of the many techniques I used to imbue the avatar with some sentience.

Since I didn't want my dear little avatar to experience vertigo, I applied a stabilizing force on the avatar's head. As the avatar zoomed around the world (banking, bobbing, weebling and wobbling), its head stayed upright, as if to be always trying to keep a stable view onto the world. Imagine what happens when you pick up a doll, an action figure like GI Joe, or a Barbie doll. If you wag the doll around in the air, the head stays rigidly-oriented on the torso. But if the doll were alive, it might tilt its head so as to keep its view on the world stable as you wobbled it around, as shown at the bottom of this illustration:

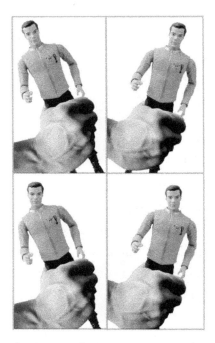

Keeping a level head creates the illusion of sentience (Image: Ventrella)

Holding a doll that adjusts its head as if it were alive might seem a tad macabre, like a scene from the *Twilight Zone*. But this image provides an example of one technique for making animated characters appear more sentient. A feature of living things is the desire to keep a stable perspective on the world. The way an avatar holds its head can create an illusion of *sentience* (which is a prerequisite for *expressiveness*).

Holding the head upright is a variation on the theme of holding the body up, which is a variation of the erect verticality of the human posture. Slithering horizontally like a lizard is one way to come across as non-human-like. Slumping in the presence of others is bad form. The postures of attractive, persuasive, and charismatic people are often perky and vertical. Thus, the visual language of verticality, perkiness, and upright posture can be designed into avatar systems, just as they are in film character animation, to create different personalities and moods.

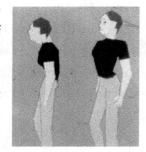

Image: Ventrella

But enough with this heady discussion. It's time to move on to the next stage of avatar evolution, and to bring the avatar into the realm of standard character animation.

Full body Articulation

The last important phase of anatomical evolution was creating a way to represent the motions of the parts of the avatar with one overarching scheme. The avatar already had ambulating legs and an articulated head. Soon our avatar had acquired two simple arms, and a few spine joints. Now the avatar had joined company with others in the world of standard character animation: it acquired a *hierarchical skeleton*. In hierarchical modeling, a "root node" or "parent node" provides the mathematical coordinate system from which all the "child nodes" rotate, in trickle-out fashion. So you could characterize the entire configuration of your body at any particular time as a list of the rotations of all your joints.

The typical modern avatar has a root, pelvis, left hip, left knee, left ankle, right hip, right knee, right ankle, torso, chest, neck, head, left clavicle, left shoulder, left elbow, left wrist, right clavicle, right shoulder, right elbow, right wrist. That makes a total of 19 joints. Some systems have fewer joints, some have more. The Second Life avatar uses this set of 19. The segments between these joints are often called "bones". Standard character animation is accomplished by dynamically translating and rotating the root joint in the global coordinate system, and also dynamically rotating all the joints in their local coordinate systems (parent-relative). So, for instance, when you walk your avatar around, you are translating and rotating the pelvis joint in the world coordinate system. As the avatar walks, the various joints branching off of the pelvis are rotated in their local coordinate systems according to a looping walk cycle.

But as we will see in chapters to come, it is not quite enough to use plain hierarchical modeling to represent the many kinds of motion required for sentience, expressivity, and interaction with the environment. Head stabilizing and leg inverse kinematics are just two examples of *procedural animation*: the various techniques that employ running software to animate, adjust, and modify motion. This is all for the sake of laying the groundwork for building a virtual human that is not only responsive to the environment, but also responsive to other virtual humans.

The Face

For many computer game or virtual world designers, it would be considered overkill to simulate the minute mechanisms of eyeballs and eyelids in their characters. It may seem a bit much to give each eyeball a full rotation matrix, or to control eyelids with variable levels of openness, or to map eyelid geometry to conform to a radius slightly greater than that of the eyeball, or to render the iris and pupil positions and rotations according to their corresponding eyeball rotations. On the other hand, this is completely justified for any avatar system that aims to be socially oriented, especially if it involves camera close-up views. For the There.com avatar prototype, the mathematics of eyeball rotation was implemented because direction of eye gaze creates a visual signal that is easily detected, and critical for clear communication. In fact, from the standpoint of avatar expressivity, an avatar skeleton representation could easily include eyeballs as *joints* (and this is sometimes done in character animation systems). As skeletal joints go, eyeballs would rank pretty darn high on the expressivity scale.

The facial rendering of the avatar for There.com went through several iterations. In design meetings, I advocated a more cartoony, flat-shaded style in order to allow the facial features that are important for expression to be easy to read. Also cartoon faces can do expressive things that real faces cannot.

Prototype avatars with cartoon-shading (Image: Ventrella)

But my prototype avatars were so cartoonlike that others found it hard to "inhabit" the avatar as themselves. Some developers experimented with making avatars that were much more realistic, with full texturing and shading. We settled on a compromise. Similar to a rendering style made popular in Pixar's films, we allowed some shading, but 'ambient light' was turned way-up, which *flattened* the rendering a bit, allowing the communicative facial delineators like eyebrows, eyelashes, lips, etc. to show up as nice crisp features.

A Colorful Evolution

There.com's avatar had a very colorful evolution—so many detours down side roads, procedural meanderings into ragdoll hell, cross-eyed bugs, exploding hair physics, and spring-loaded penises. There were also many explorations into sentience enhancements and algorithms for holding hands and other forms of avatar-to-avatar contact. Many of these inventions never made it into the final product. Such is the nature of prototyping. Below are some screenshots taken throughout the avatar's many phases.

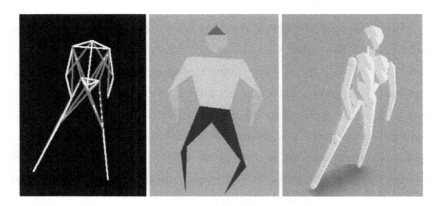

Prototype avatars using spring physics for There.com (Image: Ventrella)

Examples of prototype avatars for There.com (Image: Ventrella)

Rigging Avatars for Embodied Communication

At There.com we had debates like: "Are we building a game? Or are we building an open-ended virtual world?" Where the debate settled was that it wasn't a game: it was to be an open-ended virtual world that was socially-focused. My early prototype work in avatar expression was part of the motivation for this decision. Tom Melcher (the CEO during the company's high-growth years) used the term "Avatar-Centric Communication" to distinguish what we were doing from the existing paradigm of online virtual world communication. The trend at the time was to use disembodied text chat, with little or no connection to the 3D world that the avatars occupied. We were aiming for something new and different.

Richard Bartle, author of *Designing Virtual Worlds*, co-wrote the first multi-user-dungeon (MUD), a text-based virtual world, back in 1978. He has been a prominent authority on virtual worlds, especially in regards to the text-based variety. In describing the field of *Computer-Mediated Communication*, he says that to a specialist in the field, virtual worlds are important "...because they are media, not because they are places" (Bartle 2004). Good point...however, I'm not quite sure about his claim about "place". Now that visual virtual worlds have become established, and input devices like the Wii are bringing our bodies more intimately into these immersive spaces, virtual embodied communication is bringing "place" onto center stage. For someone like myself who came of age working on fully visual virtual worlds, the sense of place is central to experience design. This is why Will and I named our virtual world "There". It is a virtual place where the spatial aspects of bodily interaction are critical to the experience.

Avatar scholar Ralph Schroeder claims that text communication does not qualify as a form of Virtual Reality because it does not enhance—but rather, detracts from—the sense of presence and copresence. However, he acknowledges that text-chat is such a widely used mode of communication in online virtual worlds that it cannot be ignored in research on avatar communication. For the same reason, I had decided to tackle the problem of text chat in virtual worlds. Text chat was not going away; virtual worlds appeared to be growing around, or in partnership with, the already existing modalities of instant messaging and text-based virtual worlds. So the problem became: how can we build an avatar system that merges the verbal dynamics of text conversation with the sensory matrix of the 3D world in an intuitive way?

I do agree with Bartle's claim that text-based virtual worlds are more about imagination, and that graphical virtual worlds are more about the senses (Bartle 2004). I will always be imaginatively stimulated by a great novel, and possibly even more so in an online, object-oriented text-based virtual world with all the setting, character, and plot of a great novel except that it is happening in realtime all around me and I am one of the characters. But complications arise when a visual medium starts to build itself around a textual medium. To handle this media convergence, some design expertise can help.

Enter Chuck Clanton. In his busy life, Chuck has been a psychologist with a Ph.D., a medical doctor, a game designer, and a marble sculptor. Chuck and I became the two primary designers of *Avatar-Centric Communication*. In April 2003, Chuck and I gave a lecture at Stanford University (Clanton and Ventrella 2003), which was part of the Human-Computer Interaction Seminar Series, hosted by Terry Winograd. A few of the early Linden Lab engineers who created the avatar system in Second Life attended the lecture. After our presentation, they complimented us on our design ideas. They had implemented their own variations in Second Life. (In those days, the memes were flying between developers of competing startup companies like locust swarms). Since Linden Lab was culturally averse to in-house interaction design (the ugly underbelly of their successful open-ended user-generated philosophy), they didn't invest a lot of design time into these features. As a consequence, many of the avatar expression features were left undone, or under-developed. But despite this fact, and even though we at There had developed such expressivity in our avatars, Second Life had begun to build steam. Their virtual economic business model and the ability for users to customize the world to such a great extent were compelling prospects for potential success.

At There, Chuck and I had developed several techniques for adding layers of non-verbal communication to our socially-focused virtual world. I contributed several components including the automatic formation of chat groups based on the spatial arrangement of avatars. Chat balloons appeared over the avatars' heads as a way to make communication more *embodied*. I also developed techniques for controlling gaze between avatars in the group. Below is an illustration from an early prototype demonstrating gaze, as well as the early version of the chat balloon system.

An early prototype for Avatar-Centric Communication (Image: Ventrella)

The illustration also shows a user interface referencing the function keys of a standard keyboard, for triggering expressions. These keys were adapted as puppeteering triggers for body language. I had hoped that we could define a standard for using special keys on the keyboards for puppeteering avatars. This was inspired by a music education software package I once saw that came with an overlay for the computer keyboard that turned it into a simple piano. We had also explored the idea of using different "palettes" of expressions that the user could switch between for different conversational modes.

Will had hired Ken Duda to become Chief Technology Officer, and Ken started to build a team to develop the networking code, using the prototype that I was building and re-implementing it as a distributed simulation. Meanwhile, I kept prototyping new ideas. I developed some "helper" code that allowed an avatar to wander in the world as if it were being controlled by a user, using a simple AI program. In doing so, I could set my avatars wandering about, stopping in front of each other, and emitting make-believe chats for each other. This allowed me to start testing out various socializing tools that I began to work on with Chuck. These were the beginnings of our Avatar-Centric Communication System.

Analogous to the creation of Chat Rooms in traditional instant messaging systems, we wanted to allow users to create chat groups implicitly, simply by walking up to each other, facing each other, and starting to type text. These actions would be picked up by the system, and a chat group would be automatically created. Similar designs have been described by other developers and researchers, such as the Conversational Circles of Salem and Earle (2000), shown here.

Conversation Circles (Image: Ben Salem)

On the next page is another illustration of my prototype, in which you can see several graphical elements. These were used to help design the system and see all the inner-workings so that we could debug as we went along. The existence of a chat group is indicated by a "hula hoop" that encircles the group. A two-person group can (barely) be seen in the distance. My avatar (I'm the black woman in the foreground, to the left) has just joined the group of five avatars in the foreground. A small bit of my chat group's hula hoop can be seen behind my avatar. If my avatar were to move away from the center of my group, the hula hoop would grow a bit to accommodate my change in positioning, but only up to a point; if I moved far enough away, I would pop out of the chat group, and the hula hoop would shrink back to a smaller size, still encompassing the remaining five members of the group.

Prototype for chat group dynamics (Image: Ventrella)

But why did we want the software to automatically keep track of chat groups? We wanted to help the conversation along. We had two ways of doing this: camera view, and chat balloon positioning. Refer to the illustration again, in which my avatar has just joined a chat group. As soon as my avatar joined, my camera viewpoint shifted so that the heads of all the avatars in that group were in view. Also, the chat balloons of the avatars automatically lined-up from left-to-right, and became more legible. This is explained further in the chapter, "Ectoplasm".

A dotted white line is shown indicating the fact that my avatar's gaze is fixed to the head of another avatar. This avatar is my "lookat target". I would trigger this gaze behavior by passing my mouse cursor over the head of that avatar (which causes a circle to appear) and then clicking on the circle. My avatar's gaze would become "fixed" to that avatar's head. Both that avatar and my avatar could then move around within the chat group, and my head and eyes would remain fixated on that avatar's head (as long as my head didn't have to turn too much). I will explain more of this interaction and some of the considerations and consequences of virtual gaze later in this book, in the chapter called "The Three-Dimensional Music of Gaze".

The illustration is full of information. It shows how many of the aspects of Avatar-Centric Communication came together in an early stage. Because embodied communication is naturally multimodal, we realized that we had to solve many of these problems together, simultaneously, in an integrated way. This kind of design problem cannot be solved in a linear, piecemeal fashion.

On the next page is another image from the prototype, showing a different arrangement of chat balloons and avatar gaze.

Prototype for chat group dynamics (Image: Ventrella)

The Cinematographer

In most 3D virtual worlds and computer games, there is a virtual camera that follows your avatar around and makes sure it is always in view: the *third-person view*. In most virtual worlds, we spend a lot of time looking at our avatars' back-sides. That doesn't happen so much in films when we're watching the protagonist go through some adventure. As I suggested earlier, this viewpoint is a carry-over of the navigation style of many 3D games in which the player runs around in a 3D environment. In an action adventure game it's more important to look where you are going, and what lies ahead, than to watch your own face. At There, we were looking for ways to escape from some of these constraints, and the most obvious place to look was *cinema*. The virtual camera is an ever-present point of view on the world. It is usually unnoticed until it does something wrong—like getting stuck behind a tree or a wall, which obscures your view of the avatar. Virtual cameras in games and virtual worlds were initially slow to evolve cinematic intelligence, while other aspects (such as 3D modeling, texturing and lighting) have been steadily advancing at a good clip. But cinematic intelligence is now becoming more sophisticated. This is partly due to the third-person camera and the need to see your avatar as it does more complicated things than just run through a dungeon and kill monsters.

One technique developed in the early days of There.com was *two-person chat camera* behavior. It works like this: when the avatar's camera detects the initiation of a two-person chat, it *dollies* over to take a place perpendicular to the social link between the chatting avatars. This essentially places the chatters to either side of the field of view, and allows their chat balloons to take positions side-by-side.

The camera shifts to a perpendicular view for two-person chat (Image: Ventrella)

Easy enough to deal with two avatars, but how should the camera catch the correct view on a large group of avatar chatters? This presents a more complex problem to the camera. Entire Ph.D. dissertations have been written on autonomous, intelligent camera behavior—it ain't easy. I was determined to make the camera do the right thing so it could be invisible to the user—like cameras are supposed to be. While prototyping the automatic chat group system, I struggled with the following problem: when an avatar joined a chat group, how could I make the avatar's camera shift from rear-view to a view that would reveal as many faces in the group as possible, and not have any of them overlap? In coming up with a solution, I tried to make the camera shift as little as possible so as to maintain visual context (not swinging 180 degrees to the other side, for example!) Also, the algorithm was designed to try to catch as many front views of faces as possible. This scheme worked like a charm when the number of avatars in the group was small (up to about five), but things became overwhelmingly complex when the number of avatars became larger—especially since avatars tend to shift around constantly.

During play testing, some of the subjects being tested were already familiar with third-person view cameras, having played many 3D computer games. They were in the habit of shifting their avatars around—which caused their cameras to move in response. They had developed their own scheme for finding a good view. But the camera system I wrote was supposed to take care of this automatically! Since it had become so engrained in the users to move their avatars, they would unwittingly trigger the camera to *re-adapt*—often messing up their view :(This caused a continual fight between my camera algorithm and the user. As is the case with most fights between an artificial intelligence and a human intelligence, the human won. We removed this feature.

Chat Props

Chuck contributed many solutions to these problems I have been describing, based on his background in applying cinematic technique to games—such as using camera close-ups on the face. He developed some techniques that allowed the close-up face view to switch between avatars as they triggered expressions while chatting in a group.

So, now we had camera controls, avatar expressions, chat balloons, the formation of chat groups, and other techniques in our bag of tricks. After coming up with this hodge-podge of chat-related tools and algorithms, we decided that it would be best to bundle them into specific places and times when conversation was a priority (and not let them get in the way when, for example, a user is more interested in navigating a hoverboard over the hills). We called our scheme "chat props". A chat prop is a designated environment where you expect your avatar to do *conversational things*. It could take the form of a couch, a couple of stumps for seats, a stage, a café bar, or a park bench.

In *The Psychology of Cyberspace*, John Suler discusses the utility of virtual props for conversation in The Palace (an early virtual world originally developed by Jim Bumgardner for Time Warner Interactive in the mid '90s). "...props make interacting easier and more efficient by providing a visual means to express oneself. They are very useful communication tools. On the simplest level, they act as conversation pieces. If you can think of nothing else to say, express an interest in someone's prop. Talking about props is one of the most common topics of discussion at The Palace. It greases the social interaction, especially with people whom you are meeting for the first time. It's like discussing the weather—except people are more personally invested in their props than they are in whether it's rainy or sunny" (Suler).

Imagine walking down a street alone on your way to a party. You are not socializing while you are walking, although you may throw an occasional smile or "hello" to a passerby on the street. You arrive at the party and look around. Perhaps you exchange a few words with some friendly strangers, but nothing especially conversational is happening. Then you notice two friends sitting on a couch eating chips, and so you sit down with them. You choose to sit next to a friend that you particularly like. Some small talk starts up along with some starter body language. Some new brain chemistry is probably stirring around in your skull.

This regime is what we implemented in code to help structure the avatar communication activities. After your avatar is placed into a chat prop, your avatar metamorphoses into a social butterfly. Various forms of body language are created when you enter text or type out emoticons. The user can control the avatar's gaze, but also the body gaze, or "directional pose", of the entire body (like looking at someone except using the whole body—which, by the way, can be the opposite of your *head* gaze, if you want, to form variations of emotional engagement). Users could trigger various gestures, facial expressions, and even trigger the formation of extra-body visual symbols, called "moodicons".

The LoveSeat

Our first chat prop was the "loveseat": a two-person bench where we imagined a couple sitting, talking, flirting, arguing, etc.

Camera views based on body pose changes in the Love Seat (Image: Ventrella)

Aspects of the chatting activities caused the camera to cut to specific positions as the avatars changed their poses. If you sat facing your partner, the camera shot would emphasize togetherness. If you turned away, it would emphasize separation. There was an "over the shoulder" shot for each avatar, a "far away view", and various views aimed at the two loveseat sitters.

While Chuck was building the scripting tool for designing chat props, he included several parameters for configuring camera behavior like those used in the loveseat. My failed attempts at automatically orienting the camera for the best view on a conversation inspired camera settings that were opened up for the user.

Regarding some of these parameters, Chuck says, "We also gave users control over the camera so they could accept the default view on joining a conversational group, which shows everyone but is quite distant, or they could rotate and zoom the camera in to better see what they are interested in. So, for example, when seated in the audience at a stage, you can choose to have a close-up camera view of the people on the stage or of the audience or of yourself and your nearest neighbors. In some games, audience members may need to talk among themselves, which is best done with one camera, and then call out answers to someone on a stage, which is best viewed with a different camera" (Isbister 2006).

For the same reason that close-up shots are used in film (greater emotional impact), we explored using camera cuts to avatar faces when making certain expressions. This was very cool, but only up to a point. Some play-testers found that this was too jarring, and so we had to tone down the number of face-cuts. Perhaps there is no way an algorithmic cinematographer, no matter how greatly imbued with AI, can ever guess the right view on matters to match a user's needs, expectations, and communications.

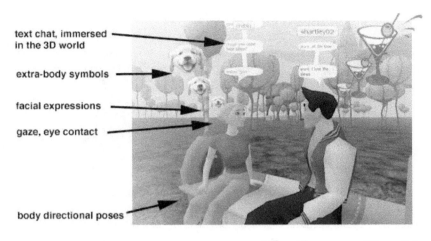

text chat, immersed in the 3D world

extra-body symbols

facial expressions

gaze, eye contact

body directional poses

Components of Avatar-Centric Communication (Image: There.com and Ventrella)

Away From Keyboard

Let's return to this theme of presence again. If a user has to step away from his or her computer, some avatar systems provide a way to indicate that he or she is "away from the keyboard" (AFK). In There.com, a visual symbol on your avatar's head makes this readily apparent to other users. A symbol (the goggles on the avatar's face in the next illustration) shows that you are away. It can be set either directly by a user or else by having the user's cursor outside of the There.com window.

The problem of representing the fact that you are AFK is familiar to most users of virtual worlds and online games. The indicators of AFK can take on many forms—some quite amusing. AFK takes on a whole new meaning when playing a game such as World of Warcraft, where critical, highly-focused gameplay has to be interrupted by a mundane need to visit the bathroom (this has come to be known as "bio-break", sometimes expressed in a chat message as "brb bio").

Avatar goggles signify that the user is *busy* (Image Jeremy Owen Turner)

In Second Life, if a user has not touched the keyboard for a while, the avatar slumps over forward as if to fall asleep while standing—or, depending on interpretation, as if it were about to lose its dinner. Here is an example of a well-intentioned idea using what some may argue is a bad choice in visual indicators. This is parodied in a video found on YouTube (Lavenac 2007) shown below, where real people act out the antics of Second Life avatars. Also shown is a parody of the default animation that plays when a user is typing text chat; the avatar acts as if she is typing at an invisible keyboard.

Video satire of avatar antics in Second Life (Image: Lavenac, 2007)

What is the best indicator for AFK? Well, it really depends on the context, and the nature of the game or virtual world. It's one thing for the user to switch on an explicit indicator of AFK, with an indication of reason ("gone fishin'", "bio-break", "astral projecting", "computer crashed", "reading the manual", etc.) before departing the virtual world to attend some other world—this is a deliberate mode change. But having the avatar system decide automatically when the user has not touched the keyboard long enough to automatically set this mode—that's not so clear. What's the right length of time? No good answer, unfortunately.

Competing Worlds

Let me pause here for a moment and insert some narrative so as to avoid confusion. Before starting this book I was told by a potential agent that I should write a juicy page-turner about the people behind There.com—its rise and fall. I told him I didn't want to write that kind of book. All I will say is that two years after working at There.com, I joined Linden Lab, makers of Second Life. So, in this chapter, and in chapters to come, I will continue telling stories about the adventures of avatar development...in the context of *both* of these virtual world companies. Aside from a few jabs here and there, I hope these accounts will come across as generally ☺☺cheery☺☺. And in some instances these stories may be strange and amusing, as in the curious case of the avatar who *slumped* while *gesticulating*—read on.

Subtleties of AFK

Both There and Second Life use avatar code that detects when the user has not pressed any keys on the keyboard for a specified duration—and when that duration passes, the avatar goes into AFK mode. While working on voice-activated gesticulation for Second Life (more details to come in the chapter, "Voice as Puppeteer"), I encountered an amusing yet annoying problem. When using voice chat as opposed to text chat, users tend not to be typing into the keyboard as much (obviously). And so, while the users were talking, their avatars would fall into slump-mode quite frequently—even through there were voices coming out of them! And since I was working on the gesticulation system, it got even weirder: these avatars would gesticulate *even while slumping!*—shoulders tilting, hands flapping, and heads bobbling. I was already not fond of Second Life's slump pose—but when I saw this anomaly, I came to dislike it even more. The solution was of course to add an extra bit of code that detected when there had been no voice signals for a specified duration, as well as keyboard activity.

In the movie, *Avatar*, Jake Sully controls his genetically-engineered Na'vi avatar while lying motionless in a sleep-like state. It's a familiar science-fiction avatar puppeteering scenario: *total brain interface*; we've seen it in *The Matrix*, and in several other films and sci fi novels. In this case, avatar control requires no body movement at all. In fact, any body movement that Jake Sully made seemed to spell trouble: if he stirred and woke up, his avatar collapsed into a heap! In this film, the equivalent of being AFK is pretty easy to detect. That's actually integral to the plot of the film. But it may not be the best AFK affordance to use in most virtual worlds or games. What is the deep solution to the AFK problem? There is no single solution. And at the same time, there are several solutions, each of which depend on context. This is just one of those problems that comes with having an avatar with an identity leash longer than zero.

Automatic Lookat

Body language can either be deliberate and conscious, or automatic and unconscious (which is usually the case). Body language habits that are unconscious can be made conscious, and later, acted out deliberately. This fact about our real selves is played out in the cloudy, chaotic world of avatar design. Here's a question: should the gaze behavior of avatars be automatic? For me, the answer is subtle and controversial. At There.com, the extended Avatar-Centric Communication team decided to add some automatic lookat features. For instance, when your avatar joins a chat group, all the other avatars automatically look at your avatar.

Conversational gaze in There.com (Image: There.com)

This tends to make users feel acknowledged and welcome. There.com avatars do these nearly subconscious social acts as part of their autonomic behavior, and it makes conversations feel much more natural. Also, if you mention the name of one of the avatars in your text chat, that avatar will automatically look at your avatar. And if you are doing most of the chatting, the other avatars will end up looking at you more than others. If you use the word "yes" or "no" in your chat, as well as other words with clearly-associated expressions, your avatar will generate those expressions nonverbally.

These automatic behaviors lend a sense of ease and social connectedness to the There experience. But in fact I have always been just a bit uneasy about these features, because the net effect, while I am operating my avatar, is that I am not entirely in control of my avatar's body language. The real issue in avatar autonomic design is not what level of body language is exactly right (they're all appropriate for different reasons). Rather, what is important is the ability to easily move between automatic and manual body language modalities—to dynamically change the length of DiPaola's leash. At the end of the day—as far as I'm concerned—a user must always be able to set his or her avatar gaze to anything or anyone, and at any time—to override the autonomic system.

The End of an Era: the Beginning of an Era

As I write these words (2010) There.com is officially closed. When a company owns a world, that world vanishes when the company folds—along with the rich virtual lives built by its residents over the years. The phenomenon of large virtual communities losing their world, and being forced into exodus to new virtual worlds, is covered by Celia Pearce in *Communities of Play* (2009). The shut down of There.com was not the first time such a tragedy has occurred. In fact, in 2004 There.com itself hosted a group of nearly 500 refugees who migrated from the defunct Myst-based game Uru. Pearce chronicles this migration in her book.

Segue

Avatar-Centric Communication is an integrated design solution addressing the problem of text communication using an avatar. Little did I know when I made that first crude cylinder moving around on a grid that things would get so complicated, and so fast. And yet, at There.com, we had only scratched the surface in terms of designing tools for embodied communication in virtual worlds.

In chapters to come, I will be filling you in on other aspects of embodied communication in avatars—aspects that are interesting enough in themselves to be given their own special chapters, such as the design of text chat balloons, and avatar animation based on a user's voice. But before we look into these other aspects, I want to first discuss a fundamental issue of conducting body language over the internet. It is the part of Avatar-Centric Communication that happens behind the scenes. It is invisible, and that's the whole idea. It is the problem of how to encode nonverbal communication in a form that can be delivered and processed quickly and efficiently. I have come to the conclusion that this problem has already been figured out...by the human brain.

5

A Body Language Alphabet

While helping to get There.com started, I was focused intently on making immersive, fun, and engaging experiences. As more software engineers accumulated in the company, I found it increasingly difficult to communicate with them. Here's why: I was so hell-bent on creating an extraordinary user experience that I was blind to one unavoidable fact: the damn thing had to work *on the internet*. The internet is a messy, confusing place. In fact, it's not a *place* at all. And for real-time animation to work properly and reliably for all participants, no matter where they are physically in the real world, there needs to be a lot of machinery under the hood to make everything appear seamless, natural, and instantaneous. One key reason for this problem is *lag*. In an ideal world, all computers would be able to exchange information as quickly as it takes an impulse to travel from one side of the brain to the other. But Earth is a tad bigger than a brain, and the connectivity is continually morphing. And there are traffic jams that cause *variations* in lag—so it is unpredictable.

Those engineers were doing me, and the company, a favor. They were solving the wickedly difficult problem of building a *distributed simulation*. There is a complex enterprise of real-world message-passing that happens behind the scenes when avatars exchange text, animations, and virtual money. Regarding the components of virtual body language (gestures, facial expressions, poses, moodicons, etc), how do these get packaged up and distributed across the internet? In the last chapter, I described the basic *experiential* components of Avatar-Centric Communication for There.com. But equally important is the design of the underlying system that allows for rapid exchange of mutual body language signals—so the user experience can be *shared*. These signals need to zip through the internet as quickly as possible. Efficient encoding is required.

Components of Body Language

In identifying the basic components of body language that can be implemented in distributed virtual environments, Mania and Chalmers (1998) list six:

1. Facial expressions
2. Gaze
3. Gestures
4. Posture
5. Self-representation
6. Bodily Contact

The more dynamic of these components: facial expressions, gesture, and (shifting) gaze, are my primary focus. They constitute a relatively high-frequency traffic of social signaling, often accompanying the production of text or speech. From a technical perspective, *posture* might be characterized as a slow form of gesture, or a full-body gesture held in place serving as a background over which dynamic gestures are played. Self-representation is one of the most pervasive forms of body language in virtual worlds like Second Life, where avatar customization is extensive.

The last component in this list—bodily contact—is one of the most powerful and visceral. Bodily contact is problematic in virtual worlds for two reasons: (1) it is technically difficult, due to current state-of-the-art in procedural avatar animation and the simulation of body-to-body physics, (2) it is psychologically and sociologically complicated. When one is immersed in the virtual world, and "one with the avatar", his or her body map is *fused* with the avatar, and the illusion of physical touch is transferred quite strongly.

Consider *griefing*, the anti-social behavior common in multiplayer computer games and virtual worlds whereby the *griefer* annoys, irritates, and harasses others, for no particular reason other than the fact that he can get away with it. Griefing could become especially ugly if there is highly-realistic simulation of physical touch in avatars. Invasion of privacy is already a concern, and the added immersion that physical touch creates could aggravate the problem. This is why the physics collision behaviors of avatars in Second Life (allowing them to bump into each other) can be switched off. This is described rather geekily as the "collisionless avatar setting used for anti-griefing purposes".

But touch isn't necessarily ugly, as we all know. Full-on simulated physical touch can be the basis for some very positive and compelling interactions. And when used by consenting adults— simulated physical touch can be very erotic. But, virtual sex aside (a sprawling topic worth several books), physical touch between avatars can have more common, everyday-like uses, such as handshaking, hand-holding, high-fives, pats on the back, elbow-jabbing, and taps on the shoulder. I will discuss a few of these bodily interactions later. But for now I want to get back on to the subject of a body language alphabet.

Categories of Nonverbal Expression

I identify two general categories of non-verbal expression distributed over the internet: (1) directly-captured expressive motion, and (2) encoded body language. These are analogous to terms that Brian Rotman uses: "non-symbolic media", and "notational media" (2008). Directly-captured expressive motion (non-symbolic media) is read from the communicator's physical body in real-time, either through a video camera, or through motion-capture sensors. The resulting signals are manifested remotely and appear either as streaming video or animated movements on an avatar or some other animated visual form. The movements directly correlate with the movements made by the communicator—possibly with some delay, but *ideally* in real-time. It is the visual equivalent of voice chat—a real-time capture of the communicator's movements.

In contrast, encoded body language (an example of notational media) is visual movement which is encoded and transferred using some kind of *alphabet*. Encoded body language can take the form of a reconstruction of previously-captured gestures and poses, and even abstract visual symbols, blended together to make up composite expressions, much the way a composer might overlap orchestral sounds or the way an artist might overlap image layers in Photoshop. Also, it can be *read* or *played* any time, without the communicator actually being present. It is plastic; it can be manipulated in endless ways (i.e. sped up, slowed down, run backwards, filtered). It is not constrained by the body of the communicator in physical space and time. It is open to cinematic treatment.

Encoded body language is the basis for many highly creative and novel performative art forms, whereby expressive human movement is mediated, amplified, deconstructed, and reconstructed via computer technology. The brilliant interactive Artificial Reality environments of Myron Krueger are but one example of mixing realtime capture with encoded effects. There are many others.

Also significant is the fact that encoded body language can be performed by physically-disabled people. If you want to make your avatar give a very excited, animated presentation while doing a slide show, but the *real you* is sick in bed, you can't be expected to put on a full motion capture suit in order to perform your avatar's high energy body language. And even if you were able and willing to wear a motion capture suit, what happens when you cough, sneeze, or yawn? What if you have an uncontrollable itch in a private part? Wouldn't you prefer to be able to do these mundane, biological acts privately, and not have them projected onto your avatar while you are making a presentation to thousands of people online?

Outering What is Inner

Beethoven was not able to hear any sound (save for a constant "whistle and buzz") when he wrote one of the greatest symphonies of all time. Steven Hawking could not speak or hold a pen when he composed some of the greatest scientific explanations of all time. Likewise, there exist physically disabled character animators who are skilled at virtual body language.

Ludwig van Beethoven

Perhaps the fact that Beethoven had previously been a pianist, and the fact that Hawking had previously been able to speak and write, account for such continued brilliance after their faculties had deteriorated. It is also true of a character animator who is wheel chair-bound but was once able to dance, bound across a rocky creek, or swing on a branch. These artists' brains had acquired the ability to run simulations of reality while their faculties had been intact.

Artistic brilliance can live in the bodymind of a physically-disabled person, and still be manifested in craft, given appropriate alphabetic tools (such as musical notation or a speech synthesizer interface). However, could these forms of virtual expression be performed in real-time? It can take Hawking several minutes to answer a simple question, given his current physical constraints. Could a modern day Beethoven perform music of the complexity and expressivity of the Ninth in a realtime performance? Computer music interfaces are getting more sophisticated all the time. VJs tweak multi-channel visuals in realtime. But what are the physical, cognitive, and technical bounds to such high-bandwidth realtime expression? This question applies to remote body language puppeteering as much as any other performative medium.

I would like to imagine a future master avatar puppeteer who has suffered a debilitating stroke and is paralyzed, but who can still express in a virtual body with the finesse of Buster Keaton, Martha Graham, or Jim Carrey. This would require some kind of encoded realtime body language notation.

Now I'd like to sharpen the focus of these two definitions I have given, explore what encoded body language might look like in the future, and reflect on what that means for avatars.

A Classification

The two categories of non-verbal expression I have just described are both valid and useful. Both will continue to evolve and flourish, because both serve different—and important—purposes for internet communication. Furthermore, they are likely to spawn many hybrid forms, which I'll discuss later. But right now let's delve into these definitions a bit more. Directly-captured expressive motion, while it may require sophisticated technology, has a more straightforward purpose than encoded body language. It must always strive to be as high-res and high-rate as possible so as to broadcast the communicator's realtime energy with verisimilitude. It is not a *language*: it is a *broadcast technology*—with the goal of re-constituting actions happening in a remote location.

Encoded body language, on the other hand, does not have this constraint, for the same reason that the written word is not constrained to the spacetime of its ancestor medium: acoustic sound. But this concept is subtler and harder to define, and still swimming in a hypothetical sea. The beginnings of a unified body language alphabet are emerging. Besides the Facial Action Coding System of Ekman and Friesen, used for simulated facial expression in games and animated films, several researchers are exploring ways to capture body language components and to classify them. This includes systems to automatically annotate body language components using cameras and a computer vision (Chippendale 2006).

Other researchers are investigating language schemes for encoding behavior across a wide range of modalities. The "Gesticon" (gesture lexicon) is a dictionary of behavior descriptions, used by the Behavior Markup Language (BML), described by Kopp et al. (2006). The BML is intended as a standard for multimodal behavior modeling in embodied conversational agents. This idea of the Gesticon has had other proposed names, such as "Gestuary", and "Gestionary" (Rist et al. 2003). Allbeck and Badler (2003) describe a "Parameterized Action Representation" to serve as a linguistic bridge between natural language and virtual agent animation. These are just a few such research projects, many of which are underway today. By the time you read this sentence, there will probably be several more notable research papers on this subject.

The illustration on the next page shows a graph with four modes of communication that I have identified. The top half refers to verbal communication and the bottom half refers to visual communication. The left half refers to directly-captured analog communication (non-symbolic), and the right half refers to encoded, symbolic, or alphabetical (notational) communication.

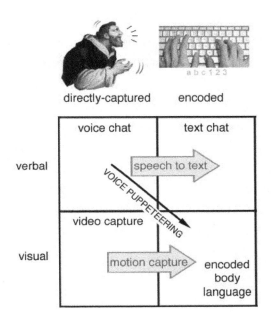

A classification of nonverbal communication modalities (Image: Ventrella)

Included in the illustration are two large arrows representing technology for capturing analog human energy and encoding it digitally: speech-to-text, and motion-capture. The diagonal arrow pointing from the voice chat quadrant to the encoded body language quadrant refers to technologies allowing a voice signal to puppeteer an avatar using an automatic gesticulation system. We'll get to this in the chapter, *Voice as Puppeteer*.

The two arrows pointing into the encoded body language quadrant represent two paths for generating encoded body language. But there are many more paths, including the various ways of triggering avatar expressions that I have been describing (through a keyboard, mouse, etc.)

Humanoid Punctuation

Text is now being used widely in conversation—circulating within the realtime interactive loop of language-generation that we find ourselves engaged in while using internet chat systems. New species of punctuation are evolving—almost by necessity, as I described earlier with the Margulian entities. Since the early days of the Medieval reading experience (I'm so glad I wasn't born then), text has acquired more and more forms of punctuation, typographic styles, and visual layout. I like to think of this as part of the ongoing evolution of encoded body language. (These earlier species are the kinds of encoded body language that are meant to be decoded within a reader's mind, so that words can be enlivened with virtual music and motion). But now that text has expanded beyond the static world of ink on paper to something more dynamic and reactive, new layers of expression and nuance are being slathered on.

The early World Wide Web emphasized textual information (and *hypertext*). Today, the internet is becoming increasingly visual and interactive. Flickr and YouTube are two examples of the surge in visual language in the era of social networking. Internet pornography has put a tweak on human sexuality due to its pervasiveness (and its covert use). The internet is becoming more like TV, cinema, games, and...dreams. Is the internet starting to wire itself directly into our limbic systems? Questions of this nature have been explored by several authors (Hayles 1999)(Kastleman 2001)(Carr 2010). The internet may in fact be more amenable to visual (rather than verbal) communication as an ecosystem of virtuality and interactivity. But I'd like to keep the focus on a specific question: given that the internet is becoming more visual and interactive, how shall we characterize the avatar within this scenario?

One view of avatars claims that they originated from computer games. They are descendents of PacMan, and have evolved to a higher dimension. Seen in this light, the avatar is a digital action figure controlled by a game player. (Note that the characters in The Sims are sometimes called "dolls"). But let's explore the avatar as a *visuo-dynamic text*—a visual counterpart to text communication. Catherine Winters suggested in a blog that "just as virtual environments like Second Life are frequently described as updated MUDs (Multi-User-Dungeons) or chatrooms, user interactions within them can be similarly enhanced by the use of body language and gestures based on that of real-world humans". In this view, the avatar provides embodiment to verbal communication. When considering the avatar as an extension of text chat, it enters the realm of language, a kind of *Humanoid Punctuation*. And since it expresses in realtime, it requires a lot more bandwidth than traditional, static punctuation.

Bandwidth

In order for us to interact intimately with each other over remote distances, the internet will have to take on significantly more data flow. Will the internet be able to physically sustain billions of simultaneous high-resolution video chat conversations? I have asked a few technical people this question, and they say that this will present no problem at all: the internet is well able to handle the load. I remain skeptical, because the human appetite for intimacy is boundless. What happens when we are able to virtualize physical touch?

But even if it is possible for the internet to handle the load, isn't it still a good idea to design more efficient ways to compress communication data?

Consider what is going on in the real world when you are engaged in a conversation with friends around the dinner table. Your eardrums are being vibrated by sound waves within a large range of frequencies (the human ear can detect frequencies ranging from about 20 Hz to about 20,000 Hz—with the human voice ranging between 300 Hz and 3000 Hz). These vibrations are converted into signals in the frequency domain, and sent down the approximately 30,000 fibers of the cochlear nerve, to the brain. While looking at your friends, billions of photons are landing on your retinas, each of which contain approximately 100 million photoreceptors. Some retinal processing goes on, resulting in signals being sent down the roughly 1.2 million nerve fibers of the optic nerve to the primary visual cortex, after being processed in the thalamus. Signals bounce around, making visits to the various players in the limbic system, and (sometimes) to areas of higher consciousness.

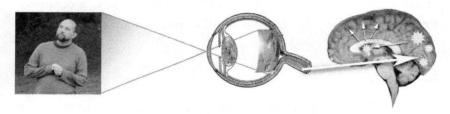

From trillions of photons to body language interpretation (Image: Ventrella)

This is a simplification of what actually happens, but it captures an important notion: we are biologically wired for data compression. There is a progressive reduction of signal density that goes on as these environmental stimuli are filtered, packaged, distilled, and re-represented where pattern recognition and prediction happen, on many levels of cortex. *Attention* helps to filter down this information further, weeding out all but the most relevant signals at any given moment. Over the span of a few seconds, trillions of environmental proto-signals will be received and processed, sometimes resulting in a response as simple as the answer "yes"—a Boolean value.

Or perhaps a nod.

Electromagnetic Expressivity

I have become a regular user of Skype—which allows voice and video calls over the internet. While *Skyping*, I expect to see my wife when we are talking long distance, and I am frustrated when the camera stops working or when the network is slow and choppy, causing my wife to turn into a Francis Bacon painting. Everyone takes telephones for granted, and now a growing wired generation is starting to take video chat for granted. The era of Dick Tracy's wristwatch has arrived—in small mobile devices.

When engaging in directly-captured body language with remote others using wireless devices, electromagnetic radiation is introduced into the sphere surrounding my body. That sphere is where natural body language generation and apprehension normally happens. Whether or not you believe this electromagnetic radiation presents a health hazard (a heavily-debated subject), there is undoubtedly room for optimization to reduce the strength of the signals. Inspiration can be found, I believe, between our ears. We can use the same processes that the

brain uses to encode and decode nonverbal signals. Do you know what would happen to your brain if the sum total of raw nonverbal sensory input were NOT reduced to efficient, bite-sized signals? It would fry like bacon. Okay, I exaggerated: but at least the smell of a hardy breakfast might become noticeable.

Natural language favors signals that zip around easily between human minds. Twitter is powerful by virtue of the 140-character limit of tweets, the quantity of tweets, and the rich social contexts within which they live. Poetry, string quartets, advertising brands, popular joke punch lines; all are examples of *memes*, where a lot of meaning is compressed into compact expressions—powerful by virtue of their brevity, mapped against the complexity of the cultural gestalts in which they thrive. This kind of relationship might be the key to how virtual body language can truly scale on the internet.

Face Caching

Even before I have met someone for the first time, I already have cached in my brain the facilities to recognize a human face—a skill I started to pick up as a newborn. Within seconds of talking to this stranger, I will have cached information about that person's appearances and behavior. As the conversation proceeds, more is cached, and I will need less focus and attention in order to gather the key attributes that make that person unique. I can then start accessing the cached representation of that person in my brain. This is much more efficient than having to continually re-apprehend this person as if I were always seeing him or her for the first time. If I have known this person for many years, I have plenty of cached memory to access, and we can engage using more brief, encoded messaging.

Compare this to an imaging technique called "super resolution reconstruction" which processes a low-resolution image—or most often a series of similar low-resolution images in a video clip—to make a derivative high-resolution image. It can be described briefly like this: imagine a ten second video of a talking head. Any single video frame might have some blur or splotch consisting of only a few pixels, corresponding to a mole or facial wrinkle. The combination of all these blurred images, each slightly shifted because the face has some movement, can be intelligently combined to resolve the detailed image of that mole or wrinkle. The dimension of time is used to determine the resulting appearance in brilliant high-resolution. This is consistent with the way human vision works—within the dimension of time. I would not be surprised if in the future, as I talk to my wife using video chat, the system will have cached attributes of her face, possibly even her body language, much the way I have in my brain. This might come to pass, not just because it is more efficient and profitable for telecom companies, or because it's a groovy technique, but because it is environmentally friendly...

Local – Global

Think globally, act locally. Here are a few (distant, but perhaps relevant) analogies. Efficient batteries are an important component in stabilizing the energy grid. Locally-stored energy can help offset the volatility of a high-demand stream of immediate-need energy. Mother Nature figured this out a long time ago by making every organism a battery of sorts. Similarly, a move toward agricultural production practices that are more distributed and local can help stabilize the food production process. Being less dependent on large-scale monoculture means less chance of large-scale invasion of pests and contaminations, and the subsequent need for high-tech, environmentally-risky solutions. The current scale of food and energy production and distribution is impacting the global environment. While human communication currently doesn't appear to be having any such effect, that doesn't mean that it wouldn't in the future. Most of us want continual buckets of love, attention, intimacy, friendship, and social intercourse. If human communication continues taking on more technologically-mediated forms—with demands for higher resolutions—then we may be in for more communication traffic jams in the future. And it may even have an environmental impact.

The solution might look something like the solutions to food and energy distribution: offsetting unsustainable centralized systems by making them more distributed and local. In the next several decades, we will see increasing decentralization in all areas, including human interaction. Ray Kurzweil takes this idea to the extreme in *The Singularity is Near*: "The ability to do nearly anything with anyone from anywhere in any virtual-reality environment will make obsolete the centralized technologies of office buildings and cities" (2005).

Bit Torrent, the peer-to-peer internet file sharing protocol invented by Bram Cohen, is an example of a successful decentralizing system. With Bit Torrent, huge monolithic data files are splintered off into manageable chunks and distributed to several locations. This swarm of chunks organically flows through the internet's irregular terrain, and makes its way to all the locations that requested the data file, reconstituted in-whole. All the participating computers use a common and efficient protocol to gather the data. Something along these lines might be the best way to distribute shared virtual reality.

Shared Reality

Shared reality does not require each participant to have a duplicate copy of the trillion-jillion-gazillion-petabyte database of human experience. Consider that a small handful of phonemes can be combined to generate the words of speech. This is tiny compared to the number of possible words and the number of legitimate ways of combining those words. In linguistics this is called "double articulation". Regarding text, the number of characters, punctuation symbols, words, and rules of usage for their combination is small compared to the number of possible sentences, poems, novels, and books about avatar body language or intestinal health that have been, or could be, written. Borges' Library of Babel is astronomically large compared to any conceivable alphabet.

Sharing an alphabet is what makes it work—for constructing words as well as for generating visual communication. A quick series of subtle overlapping avatar gestures, no matter how complex, can be triggered remotely with just a handful of bytes sent across the wires. As long as both the sender and the receiver have the appropriate code and avatar assets on their local clients, all they need to do is send the right signals between each other to invoke the right gestures, and share the experience. You can think of the common knowledge and common experiences that human brains share as our model. Like brains, all of our local computers—our viewports into a shared virtual reality—have a set of identical software components cached. Given the right amount of shared context, it would only take a few bits to create a complex experience—identical to all viewers.

I am reminded of Nicholas Negroponte's oft-quoted reference to the *wink* he expressed to his wife across the table at a dinner party (as I remember him describing it during one of his Media Lab lectures). This wink prompted a knowing grin from his wife because of an experience they had recently shared. All it took was one bit (the wink), and a wash of memories and emotions were evoked. A single wink-bit could also create a connection to the current topic of conversation, placing it in a new context, and conveying an enormous amount of information—100,000 bits-worth. This metaphor has been used to argue that higher network bandwidth is overrated as a necessity (Fiber-optics! Faster speeds! Bigger pipes!)

Wrong: *Smarter* communication.

Two brains with common experience can communicate efficiently (Image: Ventrella)

Local computers that we use to log into current virtual worlds are typically *clients* in a *client-server* architecture. The server acts as a normalizer through which communication happens. And any web developer or virtual world software engineer will tell you: the more efficient and leaner you can make the data communications over the internet, the better off you are. What better model is there than cognition to use as a guide for making believable, immersive, and expressive virtual worlds?

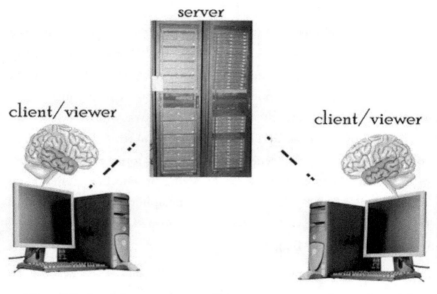

Clients with shared data can use more efficient communications (Image: Ventrella)

Maturana and Varela's rejection of the "tube metaphor" of communication (1998) is worth mentioning here. According to the tube metaphor, communication is generated at one point (the sender), transmitted through some conduit (like a tube), and then it ends up at a destination point (the receiver). A United States Senator famously described the internet as "a series of tubes" (Stevens 2006). This is not an accurate way to characterize internet ecology—or communication in general. Maturana and Varela prefer a characterization that acknowledges the behavioral dynamic of a whole organic system. Communicative actions may not necessarily follow such clear explicit paths. Also, *information* is not inherent in the stuff that passes through the tube; it is "created" by the receiver. Similarly, the communicative scenarios I have been describing derive meaning not from what passes through the *tubes of the internet*, but from the way these sweet little efficient packets trigger behavioral changes in a social environment.

Microgestures

Now, back to the body language alphabet. Birdwhistell (who coined the term "kinesics") suggested that the smallest unit of body language should be called the "kine". Referring to the progressive building-up of body language structures, he used terms like "kineme" (analogous to *phoneme*), "kinomorph", and "kinomorpheme" (Birdwhistell 1970). For simplicity, let's just call our elemental units "microgestures". These are atomic, nameable building blocks of body motion that can be combined in series and overlapped in many ways to produce all the familiar non-verbal signals that we use every day.

A leftward cock of the head; eyes glancing upward; eyes glancing to the right; shoulders slumping; a clenched right fist; a slightly-suppressed smile; a stare with eyelids slightly peeled; a step back on the left foot; puffing-out the chest; furrowing the brow; nose-puckering. The list is long, and yet we could probably settle on about a hundred such micro-gestures to treat as *atoms* that can be cobbled together to make exponentially more gestures of more complex non-verbal expression. Even these could be broken down into smaller components. A clenched fist is really a combination of many finger joints bending. It's all a matter of what level of detail we want to use as our base representation.

We may also refer to the facial action components logged by Paul Ekman and Wallace Friesen that can be combined in various ways to make any facial expression (Ekman et al. 1984). In fact, let's incorporate this list into our imagined set of micro-gestures. We could probably fit an enumerated list of well-defined microgestures into a single byte: 256 possible values—each value serving as an index for a unique microgesture. By combining groups of these microgestures, we could produce almost any imaginable nonverbal expression. The English alphabet has 26 letters. The ASCII standard of character representation adds some punctuation, symbols and control characters, making the set larger. The Unicode standard encoding UTF-8 uses one byte for the ASCII characters, plus up to 4 bytes for other characters. Our body language alphabet could easily fit into a package of a few bytes. Let's throw in a few extra bytes related to timing (i.e., start time plus duration), blending options, and amplitudes. And then let's add a few other parameters determining how the alphabet forms the nonverbal equivalent of words, sentences, and phrases. Sending a few bytes over the internet every second is nothing to blink at these days. And so, it is easy to imagine a compact, efficient protocol for delivering rich body language in real-time.

Of course, this is not the whole picture. If the goal is to build a system that generates meaningful behavior from an encoding, just defining the primitive elements is not enough. Some higher-level filtering, representation, and modeling has to take place. For instance, gestures can be divided into categories, such as those defined by McNeill (1996): *iconics* (gestures that bear resemblance to the thing being talked about), *metaphorics* (describing abstract things), *deictics* (pointing movements referencing spaces, things, concepts, and directions), *cohesives* (gestures that tie together thematically related ideas that become separated in time due to the nature of speech), and *beats* (movements that mark particular words for emphasis). We may consider postural stances, which are often unconscious and can indicate emotion, and *emblems*, which are like visual words (i.e., flipping the middle finger, thumbs-up, salute, etc.) Having higher-level representations like these, as well as established notations, could provide a framework of grammatical rules for piecing together the alphabetical components.

More Rationale for Encoded Body Language

Since humans are able to recognize and process analog communicative gestures, expressions, and postures as semantic units, it seems natural that we should use a similar kind of scheme to deliver body language online. Employing an alphabet and a grammar is more efficient than cramming as many video pixels or 3D model polygons as possible into the pipe as fast as possible to transmit the details of a remote expressive event.

And even though motion-capture techniques can result in data that is more efficient than pixels or polygons, it is still a mere non-linguistic recording of pure movement. Michael Kipp and his research colleagues explain that while these kinds of processes "...result in fine grained, purely descriptive and reliably coded data which can be reproduced easily on a synthetic character, the annotative effort is immense. In addition, the resulting data is hard to interpret. It does not abstract away even minor variations and the amount of data is so massive that it is hard to put it in relation to the accumulated knowledge about gesture structure and form found in the literature". (Kipp et al. 2007) With this in mind, Kipp, and others, have been exploring ways to capture the essential temporal and spatial aspects of conversational gesture and annotate them in a form that can be efficiently re-created on an animated character.

Analog – Digital – Analog

I recently typed the word "Bancouver" into a text document when I meant to type "Vancouver". Since I'm not a touch typist and have to watch the keys most of the time, many typos can go unnoticed. The worst is when I accidentally hit the caps-loCK KEY AND DON'T REALIZE IT'S DOWN UNTIL I LOOK UP AT THE SCREE...damn, there I go again. Regarding "Bancouver", I noticed later that *B* is sitting right next to *V* on my keyboard—a mere centimeter away. This is an easy mishap when a literary twitch comes out that may have been more productive in the gestural expression space...

The reason is that gestures are analog. Alphabets are digital. This particular error would not happen in the gestural space of speech and body language. Perhaps a labial twitch could create a *B* sound instead of a *V* sound while discussing Canadian politics over beers (especially several beers). Or perhaps this would be the result of an accent or a language translation. And in terms of bodily expression, a wave of the hand in a northerly direction while referencing Vancouver would not suffer the same kind of "typo" if there were a one-centimeter twitch of a finger.

Animal communication signals can be classified as either *discrete* or *graded*. Discrete signals are either on or off, and are more clearly marked in time. Graded signals can vary over time. They have fuzzier boundaries, and can carry subtle tones of meaning. Discrete signals naturally translate to symbols. Graded signals less so. A rapid uttering of short, discrete sounds over time can result in a subtle, graded-like signal, such as some forms of traditional polyrhythmic African music, the phasing texture of Steve Reich's music, or the electronic music of Aphex Twin (where superfast rhythms blur into gestural phrases).

The 1s and 0s which are the atoms of computing are discrete (as discrete as you can get). When people describe computers in terms of being "just ones and zeros", they are correct only on one level (like, the lowest). That is certainly not what computers are about, any more than you and I are "about" carbon, hydrogen, and oxygen. The signals that computers generate, while digital on the smallest scale, are dedicated to creating analog experiences for us. These signals have reached such blinding speeds and high bandwidths that they create a blur. In virtual world craft, that's intentional. We experience the illusion of analog space and time, movement, and sound—graded signals.

One take-away from this is that all signaling, whether of a discrete or graded nature, can be represented digitally. That makes everything ultimately "alphabetizable", i.e., manipulable as notational media (*including* motion capture).

Notation of human movement is what *Labanotation*—a system originating from the work of dance theorist Rudolf Laban—is centered on: capturing essential aspects of human movement, for choreography, athletics, physical therapy, and many other domains. This general notion of *alphabetizing human movement* brings us back to the ideas of Brian Rotman that we touched upon earlier...

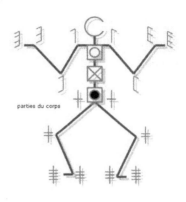

Labanotation (Wikimedia Commons)

The Alphabetic Body

The alphabet and the written word have shaped modern civilization and serve as its dominant *cognitive technology*. But alphabetic texts do not convey the bodily gestures of human speech: the hesitations, silences, and changes of pitch that infuse spoken language with affect. Only to a very small degree do our current handful of punctuations achieve this. Some people believe that speech-to-text processing software is replacing the act of writing as we know it. But why just stop at the actions of our "speech organs" (tongue, teeth, lips...)? Brian Rotman proposes a kind of *gesturo-haptic writing* as a whole-body form of communicating. "...why not notate the movement of any and all the body's organs and parts, aural or otherwise, signifying and a-signifying alike?" He proposes bringing the body back into writing—the "alphabetic body" (2008).

Let's riff on Rotman a bit. Speech-to-text processing software receives the analog sounds of your voice as input, interprets them as a string of words, and types them into a text editor immediately after you utter the words. The sound of the voice—phonetic speech—is an analog signal that is converted into a digital signal (based on an alphabet). Whole-Body Annotation takes this idea to its logical extreme. Again, why just use the voice as input? Video cameras could also be capturing the gestures, facial expressions, and gaze, and laying down a notation parallel to and simultaneous with the alphabetical text being laid down.

Let's use our proposed Encoded Body Language scheme to lay down a body language text, data-compressed for efficient internet communication. This new text layer could be hidden for normal book-like reading of the text. However, the entire text (body and all) could also be "played", using an avatar or some other dynamic visual medium to reconstitute the whole-body expression.

Could this scenario ever be realized? Not sure. The point is: a body language alphabet is reasonable, logical, and possible. We already have a very limited form of body language notation (written text—which codifies phonetic speech). Seeing speech as a limited form of body language allows us to extrapolate to the whole body—and it starts to make more sense. The existence of avatars and the likelihood of their future ubiquity as a *visual text* makes this idea that much more convincing.

6

The Uncanny Valley of Expression

A virtual Marilyn Monroe was developed in the '90s at MIRALab, University of Geneva, headed by Nadia Magnenat-Thalmann. Virtual Marilyn has been used as subject matter for many computer graphics experiments, including simulating the physics of clothing. The image below shows Marilyn from a scene in the video Rendez-vous in Montreal.

Virtual Marilyn from a scene in the video Rendez-vous in Montreal (Image: Thalmann)

Images of the virtual Marilyn were impressive by the standards of the time in which they were being developed. But as lovely as virtual Marilyn may have looked in screenshots, when she was animated her artificiality became glaring and unsatisfying. The pursuit of realism in virtual humans can cause a phenomenon known as The "Uncanny Valley". This term refers to a creepy discomfort that people experience in reaction to robots or 3D animated characters that are *almost* lifelike (but not so lifelike as to fool people into thinking they are real). Masahiro Mori, the roboticist who coined the term, expressed the idea in a graph that plots the amount of positive reaction as a function of realism.

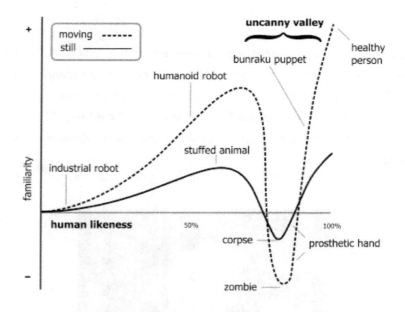

The uncanny valley graph (Image: Wikimedia Commons)

The graph shows a significant dip in human positive reaction as the robot or 3D character approaches—but doesn't quite reach—perfect realism. Sigmund Freud expounded on the idea of the *Uncanny* in an essay (1919) as an instance of something appearing familiar, yet foreign at the same time, resulting in an uncomfortable, strange feeling of cognitive dissonance. One can feel attracted and repulsed at the same time. Notice that the graph differentiates between *moving* and *still*; I will be getting into the motion aspects shortly.

Cartoon characters and abstracted images of people are easy to digest visually. The human eye-brain fills in the details and incorporates them into a comfortable internal representation, a notion articulated famously in *Understanding Comics* by Scott McCloud (1993). But when there is too much detail, less is left up to interpretation. Anything missing or visually inaccurate becomes obvious. Suspension of disbelief goes out the window. Using non-human representations is one way to avoid the uncanny valley. Animator Chuck Jones preferred using animals in his cartoons, claiming, "…it is easier and more believable to humanize animals than to humanize humans" (Jones, 1989).

Yee, Ellis, and Ducheneaut have explored the question of how to represent embodiment in virtual worlds, and go so far as to suggest that, far from reliably replicating physical reality, we might benefit from deliberately breaking the rules of literal representation. "As we explore and develop virtual worlds for a wide variety of applications, it is important to ask whether our insistence on replicating physical reality inadvertently means carrying along unnecessary baggage from the physical world. Indeed, we suggest that it is more fruitful to ask instead what worlds we could create if we broke those expectations purposefully" (Yee et al. 2009).

They use the illustration on the next page to show a spectrum of embodiment, and an implied range of expression and information visualization possible when the pressure for literal representation is relaxed.

Levels of abstraction for embodiment (Image: Yee, Ellis, and Ducheneaut, 2009)

Tromp and Snowdon (1997) (in a paper that bears the same main title as this book) recognized the need to start with simplistic forms of embodiment, and to include only what is necessary for expression as determined by the application purposes and the user's needs. Computing power at the time was limited, yet the authors acknowledge that there will *always* be limitations. There are practical reasons for using abstract forms of embodiment and staying focused on the problems of communication, interaction, and expression.

Obsession with realism has generated many monsters—especially when they move. Below at left is a screenshot from a video of the Japanese robot, "Repliee Q1Expo", which is almost lifelike. She looks very real in photographs, but as soon as you see her move, everything changes.

Repliee, the Japanese humanoid robot

At the right of the screenshot is a picture of Repliee nose-to-nose with a graduate student, published on the cover of a pamphlet for the Christian Science Monitor. It asks: "Which is the robot?" My response: I don't know, because it's not moving...duh! By the way, the face at the far right is real, and the bald man at the left holding the magazine is (more) real.

The uncanny valley can also be provoked by a lack of expressivity. In discussing the uncanny valley in 2006, Wagner James Au, author of *The Making of Second Life* and a popular blogger, expressed his dismay with the lack of avatar expression: "...you usually see pictures of dramatic but expressionless avatars, appealing if they're attractive or unique, but not emotionally engaging. This is frustrating to me as a virtual world journalist, trying to convey in screenshots the very real emotions that are being expressed in interviews by residents, through their text or through their builds. Occasionally, an avatar's expression does match what the person behind it is trying to convey, and it's profoundly moving" (Au 2006).

I was one of three keynote speakers at the Virtual Worlds 2000 conference. For my presentation, I discussed how the concept of "Realism" is still heavily influenced by references to High Renaissance painting. I advocated the notion of *behavioral realism* in avatars, suggesting that developers apply lessons from physics, genetics, and psychology over computer graphics rendering, in the art of avatar-making. I was also advocating a cartoony style of avatar design, to make expressions easier to read. Complexity guru Yaneer Bar-Yam was another keynote speaker. My wife and I were having breakfast with Yaneer, and we were talking about Nadia Magnenat-Thalmann's virtual Marilyn Monroe, which he referred to as "wooden". Yaneer is always interested in getting to the behavioral essence of systems, be they biological, cultural, political, neural, or mathematical.

Nadia was another keynote speaker at the conference. She was in another room while we were eating our breakfast. Yaneer decided to approach her on this issue of the uncanny valley and her wooden Marilyn. I chose to stay focused on my wife and my croissant. When Yaneer returned, he looked as if he had just come out of a blizzard in the Swiss mountains. The conversation did not go well. And it didn't help that they both have such strong personalities! I see this as just one moment of friction in a long pendulum swing from computer graphics realism to behavioral realism. I think that the pendulum is not finished with its swing, and that the swing is leaving in its wake a whole spectrum of virtual human craft.

I once had an epiphany when I saw a realistic virtual human with a clipping plane that was being used to slice it open: it became obvious that it is hollow inside. That's because 3D computer graphics models are all just empty polyhedra. This is revealed sometimes even in the most sophisticated, highly-crafted games, such as Half Life: the virtual camera, while in the midst of a hubbub of activity, will sometimes accidentally poke inside of one of the characters, revealing its utter hollowness (and sometimes the inside the head of the player's own character). The effect is jarring to say the least.

This hollowness is a reminder of the thin veil of illusion that comprises simulated humans, with current state-of-the-art virtual craft. I like to use this visual bug as a metaphor: what is missing is an underlying reason for things to look and act the way they do. My underlying thesis is that genetics, psychology, language, and physics (basic fundamental phenomena of nature) should be the driving forces for simulating humans. Not optical appearances. While this doesn't necessarily portend a complete overhaul on the avatar-making process, it does signify a paradigm-shift that can influence the development process in subtle but important ways. I am specifically interested in the fundamental first principles that cause a digital character to animate expressively. By wiring up a direct link from emotion, conversational context, and attention, to drive a character's movements, we can more easily steer clear of the uncanny valley. Let us now delve a bit deeper into the behavioral aspects of making virtual humans, with a critical eye towards visual realism.

The uncanny valley is exacerbated when there is a large difference between visual and behavioral realism. Jeremy Bailenson of the Virtual Human Interaction Lab at Stanford notes that the effect of *copresence* (the experience of being in the presence of others) is lowest when there is a mismatch between the appearance and behavioral realism of an embodied agent (Bailenson et al. 2005). When we see a realistic human-like avatar, we unconsciously expect it to do similar things that a real human would do. And we also read signals from this representation as if it were a real human. So, in the case of Catherine's avatar (which was seen as unfriendly and cold), her body language was interpreted as having meaning and intent. And this is because of the fairly realistic human representation. Visual affordance was out of proportion with behavior. I argue that when avatar designers are able to get these proportions right, they not only avoid the uncanny valley: they pass the *believability test*.

Hyper-Realism

If jaw-dropping photorealism is what avatar developers really want, then they are advised to make a shortcut: slip a human into the animation workflow, via motion-capture. And that's just the way photorealistic graphics and realistic animation has been calibrated in many recent technologies. You can't get more realistic motion than having a real person do the moving. Speaking of which, there is one thing that has been nagging me: a conversation floating around about how *amazing* virtual actors have become, and how they will put real actors out of business.

I recall reading the announcement of a system for facial animation developed by a company called Image Metrics. The announcement had some commentators chanting about how virtual actors have been taken to the highest level yet. Well, yes and no. The visual graphics of the system are synthetic, but the behavior is not synthetic, any more than the voice of Louis Armstrong that we hear etched in vinyl is synthetic. We don't question whether the voice originated from Armstrong himself, although we may not be happy with the fidelity of the recording. So, all this fuss about virtual actors being indistinguishable from real actors is misguided. They *are* real actors (driving digital puppets).

And no. Real actors are not being put out of business.

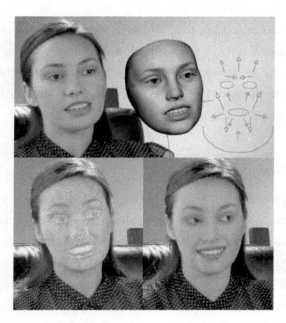

Facial animation and rendering (Image: Image Metrics – from the "Emily Project")

Hopefully, the release of the film *Avatar* will finally put this conversation to rest. Motion capture has now reached such sophistication that the original actors can shine through their digital puppets. In fact, director James Cameron prefers the term "performance capture". He claims that in *Avatar*, "110% of the actor performance came through in the final character" (Cameron 2009). This is why he used head-rigs with face cameras to capture teeth, tongue, lips, and rotations of eyeballs—all of this being done in combination with motion-capture markers on the body, and often with props and "look-at targets" within the environment, to help embed the actors' whole bodies within the environment as much as possible.

Critical, subtle nonverbal emotional nuances were recorded at high frame-rates, along with the tremors of fear and quivers of excitement that come through their voices. No question: these are real actors, and their credits in the film are justified. When we see Sam Worthington and Zoe Saldana working up towards the first kiss, while decked-out in their digital Na'vi costumes, indeed we may feel a bit uneasy with the blue skin, large yellow eyes and cat-like noses. But I would put this in a whole different psychological category—this is not *the uncanny valley of expression*. It passes the believability test.

Beyond Human

We developers of social virtual world software don't deal with high-end, actor-driven digital puppetry as a general rule. It is just not possible to gather the talent, money, or computing power to animate avatars like what we see in Cameron's film. By necessity, we have to work with less-realistic visual manifestations of user agency. But I prefer having a less visually realistic avatar anyway. The uncanny valley is completely unnecessary and avoidable in the pursuit of distributing expression and identity. Avatar designers simply need to calibrate graphical realism with behavioral realism. This is why I championed the more cartoony style of the avatars in There.com (though I did not champion the idea to have them all look like preppy

WASPS at Club Med). And it's why my avatar in Second Life is a cube of six fractal images with green tentacles hanging beneath.

Humanoid vs. abstract/surreal avatars (Image: There.com and Ventrella)

I might even go as far as to say that I would be happy if we just cast off these human visages, and took on more universal forms that resonate with all Earthlings. We are poised between animal and post-human. There is a great spectrum available to us for self-expression. Human likeness just seems so...limiting—and it is certainly problematic!

We will be exploring various non-human variations in a later chapter. But first, I want to take another look at this notion of believability in motion. In this case we will distill our representations down to a form that has no risk whatsoever of falling into the uncanny valley. We will distill our representations down to three moving dots.

7

The Gestural Turing Test

Alan Turing came up with a thought-experiment in 1950. It was intended as a way to test a machine's ability to demonstrate intelligent behavior. The Turing Test has since become one of the hallmarks of artificial intelligence (AI) research, as well as a source of continual debate. Turing had been exploring the question of whether machines can think. To avoid the difficulty of defining "intelligence", he proposed taking a behaviorist stance: Can machines do what we humans do? (1950) In the Turing Test, a human observer engages in a conversation (using text-chat only) with two hidden agents—one of them is a real human and the other is an AI program. If the observer thinks that the AI program is a real human, the AI program passes the Turing Test.

Verbal language may be the ultimate indicator of human intelligence, but it may not be the most representative indicator of intelligence in the broadest sense. Intelligence may be better understood, not as something based on a system of abstract symbols, grammars, and logical decisions, but as something that emerges within an embodied, situated agent that must adapt within a complex, dynamic environment.

Referring to the Turing Test, N. Katherine Hayles, in *How We Became Posthuman*, writes, "Here, at the inaugural moment of the computer age, the erasure of embodiment is performed so that 'intelligence' becomes a property of the formal manipulation of symbols rather than enaction in the human life-world" (1999). Hubert Dreyfus was one of the earliest and most forceful critics of AI (or, what some now call "Good Old-Fashioned AI"), claiming that a machine cannot achieve intelligence without a body (Dreyfus 1972). No doubt it is impressive that the chess-playing computer Deep Blue was able to beat Kasparov in 1997, but Deep Blue is a very specialized machine. MIT robot-master Rodney Brooks famously said, "Elephants don't play chess". "We do not usually complain that a medical expert system, or an analogy program cannot climb real mountains. It is clear that their domain of expertise is somewhat more limited, and that their designers were careful to pick a well circumscribed domain in which to work. Likewise it is unfair to claim that an elephant has no intelligence worth studying just because it does not play chess" (Brooks 1990).

Intelligence emerged out of a long evolution of brains evolving within bodies, in complex ecologies. Written language is a recent invention in the long evolutionary history of communicative behavior in the biosphere. Considering that intelligence (and therefore communication) arose from the deep evolution of life on earth, email, instant messaging, and virtual worlds came into existence in the blink of an eye. The classic Turing Test therefore addresses only a thin veneer of intelligent behavior.

Regarding the creation of AI programs, if we can simulate at least some basic aspects of the embodied foundations of intelligence, we may be better prepared to then understand higher intelligence. It might also be useful for simulating believable behaviors in computer games and collaborative virtual environments. According to Justine Cassell, while there is a trend towards ambient computing in which the computer becomes more invisible, and where background environments (like rooms in a house) become more intelligent, we still have a natural need to identify the physical source of an intelligence. Human bodies are the best example. "We need to locate intelligence, and this need poses problems for the invisible computer. The best example of located intelligence, of course, is the body" (Cassell 2001).

Artists evoke bodily intelligence (Image: Michelangelo and Ventrella)

Instead of using disembodied text as the primary messaging alphabet for a Turing Test, what if we used something more primal, more fundamental? My answer is the *Gestural Turing Test*, a variation which uses a *gestural alphabet*. Here is how it works: a human subject sits in a chair to the right of a large room divider. In front of the subject is a large screen with two sets of three moving dots. A human controller sits silently in a chair to the left of the divider, also facing the screen. The movements of the three dots on the left of the screen are either created by the hidden human (who is wearing motion capture markers on his head and hands), or by an AI agent—a computer program animating the dots algorithmically. A random decision determines whether the motions will be controlled by the human or by the AI. The subject must decide which it is. The subject is wearing the same motion capture markers as the hidden human, and understands that he is controlling the dots on the right of the screen. The subject is told that the hidden agent "sees" his motions, and will try to interact gesturally.

A schematic illustration of the Gestural Turing Test (Image: Ventrella)

Now, you may ask: what is there to discuss if you only have a few points to wave around in the air? In the classic Turing Test, you can bring up any subject and discuss it endlessly. There is just no way to discuss your grandmother's arthritis or the Civil War with three moving dots. So, what is the activity? What "game" does the subject play with dots? Well, the goal of the Turing Test is simply to fool a human subject into believing that an AI program is a human. Period. However that is accomplished is up to the subject and the AI program. Turing chose the medium of text chat, which is devoid of any visual or audible cues. Body language was thus not an option for Turing. In contrast, I propose a small set of moving dots, and no verbal communication. Moving dots are abstract visual elements (like the alphabet of written language), however, they are situated in time, and more intimately tied to the original energy of natural language.

One may argue that since we don't normally communicate with moving dots, there's not much basis to the idea of having "successful" communication using only dots. However, I would argue that the written word is just as abstract, and just as arbitrary. And don't be fooled by this number *three*. The fact that these dots move means that they are capable of an essentially infinite range of expressive motions and visual phrasings. The difficulty with considering three moving dots as a viable "alphabet" is based on the fact that we grew up with a very different alphabet: the alphabet of written language. It has permeated every corner of society, and so we don't question whether it is natural—in fact, we may not be capable of questioning it, because *verbal literacy has become our primary virtual reality*—a virtual reality by which other realities are referenced. And that includes me writing—and you reading—these words.

A Turing Test that uses body language creates a different dimension of possibilities. For instance, an AI program could be made to appear like a real person trying to communicate gesturally, as if to say, "Indeed, I am alive!" or, "Yes, I see you are gesturing at me". Perhaps the AI program could be programmed to spontaneously start playing an imitation game, which may turn into something like a geometrical question-and-answer activity. Once the personality and mood of the two agents (one human, one not) were mutually detected, the activity would become more nuanced, and certain expectations would come into effect. After extended time, it might be necessary for the AI program to interpret certain gestures semantically, to accommodate the spontaneous language genesis that the human subject would be forming. Whether or not these gestures were conscious signals given by the subject, the AI program might be designed to attribute meaning to them if they tended to occur often and in response to certain situations. Incidental motions could be used as well, such as the effects of scratching, stretching, shifting one's weight, (and other effects caused by a real human anatomy behind the dots), to lend some realism and casual believability to the experience. In fact, I would even suggest giving the AI program the option to stand up and walk off the screen, as if to say, "enough of this silly game...I'm bored". And why not? As far as I'm concerned, that is within the realm of body language allowed in the Gestural Turing Test.

Behavioral Realism

Since I am taking the Turing Test into a visual realm here, why am I proposing to use such a simple graphical representation? Why not render fully realistic virtual humans? One reason is that I want to avoid the uncanny valley. The goal is not visual realism—it is *behavioral* realism. We have plenty of examples of image-based Turing Tests— depictions of virtual humans on the covers of Computer Graphics journals and Computer Game magazines. These images are starting to become indistinguishable from photographs of real people. More and more of them are passing the "Image Turing Test".

But human eyes and brains don't use images to apprehend a Living Other—because images don't include *time*. There is another reason I have proposed to use only dots: any attempt at visual realism would constitute a distraction to the goal of the test—which is about pure motion. How much visual detail can be removed from a signal while still leaving the essence of expressive motion? This is one of the questions asked by researchers who use *point light displays*, a visualization technique that is often used to study biological motion.

Research shows that people are really good at detecting when something is being moved by a living thing as opposed to being moved by a machine or by the wind. Experiments using point light displays have been used on subjects to test perception of various kinds of motion.

Image: Ventrella

These experiments demonstrate that you don't need very many points of light for people to figure out what's going on. Researchers have even located neural structures in the brain that respond to the motions of living things as opposed to non-living things.

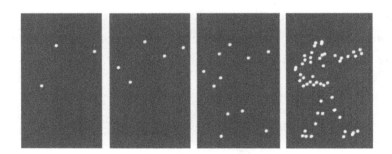

How many moving dots do you need to detect human movement? (Image: Vicon)

Believability

Variations of the Turing Test have been used as a testing methodology by several researchers to measure believability in virtual character motion (Livingstone 2006)(van Welbergen et al. 2008) – just to name a few. "Believability" is an interesting concept. Film critics refer to the viewers' suspension of disbelief. The concept is familiar to human-like robot makers and game AI designers. It plays into the world of political campaigning. Believability is in fact a fuzzy metric and it might be better to measure it, not as a binary yes or no, but as a matter of degree. It has been suggested by some critics of the classic Turing Test that its all-or-nothing criterion may be problematic, and that a graded assessment might be more appropriate (French 2009).

Consider the amount of visual detail used. Several dots (dozens, perhaps) would make it easier for the human observer to discern between artificial and human. But this would require more sophisticated physical modeling of the human body, as well as a more sophisticated AI. I propose three points: the head and hands are the most motion-expressive points of the body. These are very mobile parts of the body, and most gestural emblems originate in these regions. The graph shown below is similar to the uncanny valley graph that we saw earlier. It illustrates the following hypothesis: as the number of points used to reveal motion increases, the subject's ability to detect whether it is real or not increases. Believability goes up for real humans, and it goes down for artificial humans. Or, to put it another way, humans become more identifiable as humans and artificial humans become more identifiable as artificial.

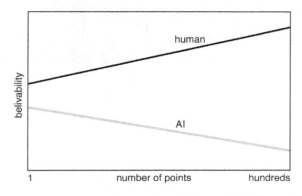

With more points it is easier to distinguish real from artificial (Image: Ventrella)

The implications of this are that the Gestural Turing Test could be deployed using many possible levels of visual realism. The more visual realism that is used, the more sophisticated the AI algorithms need to be to accommodate visual detail. *Believability* is not an absolute value or a universal constant; it varies among types of media, observers, and contexts.

The Experiment

Enough with all this pontificating, hand-waving, and thought-experimenting! In the fall of 2009, I was doing research and teaching a class at the School for Interactive Art and Technology (SIAT), at Simon Fraser University in Vancouver BC. I was working under Professor Magy Seif El-Nasr, who does research in believability and nonverbal behavior in avatars and game characters (2009). I suggested that we implement a Gestural Turing Test and she said, "Let's do it". With technical help from graduate student Bardia Aghabeigi, we put together a Gestural Turing Test using the Vicon motion capture studio at Emily Carr University of Art and Design in Vancouver (Ventrella et al. 2010). We designed a handful of AI algorithms that mimic the motions of human hand and head positions. Bardia implemented a network-based architecture allowing the AI to send motion data to the Vicon system where it could be picked up by a rendering engine and animated on a large screen, just as I explained earlier.

The modern motion-capture studio is an impressive set-up. In the studio we used, the room is large, windowless, and painted completely black. There are twenty cameras lined up at the top of the four walls, next to the ceiling. These cameras act like compound eyes that look down upon the human subjects from several viewpoints as they move about. The Vicon system pieces together the data streams from the cameras, some of which may not see all the points at times because they may be hidden from view, and re-constructs the 3D geometry. We attached motion capture markers (highly-reflective little balls) to a couple of soft hats and gloves, and configured the Vicon system to expect these markers to appear on the heads and hands of two different people, separated by several meters. We grabbed one of those large soft pads that motion capture stunt actors are supposed to fall onto and not break bones, and we propped if up on its edge as a makeshift room divider. (It served as an acoustic divider as well). We set up two chairs, each facing the huge screen that projected the computer display of the markers.

Motion capture studio with a room divider (Image: Rick Overington, ECUAD)

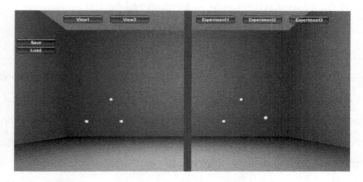

Displaying the moving dots using the Unity Game engine (Image: Ventrella and Aghabeigi, SIAT, SFU)

Gestural AI

Three hidden agents were used to drive the dots on the left side of the screen: one human and two experimental AI algorithms. The AI algorithms were quite simple as far as AI programs go. To make them look as authentic as possible, we used a "background" layer of continual movement. This was meant to give the impression of a person sitting with hands hanging by the sides of the chair, or shifting to put the hands in the lap, or having one hand move over to the other hand as if to adjust the motion capture marker. Some of these background movements included scratching an itch in some nonspecific part of the body. A barely-perceptible amount of random motion was added to make the points appear as if they were attached to a living, breathing person. This is similar to a technique called "Perlin Noise", named after Ken Perlin, who devised various techniques for adding random noise to graphical textures and synthetic motion (Perlin 1995).

The first AI algorithm used a set of pre-recorded motions as its vocabulary of gestures, and it used a simple blending scheme (the transitions between gestures were not very smooth). This was so that one of the AI programs would perform less reliably than the other, in order to give variation in believability. The other AI algorithm used an imitation scheme. When it detected movement in the subject that was over a specific threshold, it would start "watching" the gestures of the subject, then after a few seconds of this, it would play back what it "saw". It would blend smoothly between its background motions and its imitative gestures. If no movement was detected above the threshold, it would default to just playing background motions.

The Subjects

On the day of the experiment, I went out and hunted for students wandering the halls of Emily Carr University and asked them if they had ever been in a motion capture studio, and if they would like to be subjects in a psychological experiment. Most of them were eager and excited. I collected a total of 17 subjects. Each subject was invited to sit in the chair, put on the hat and gloves, and begin thinking of him or herself as a primitive avatar in the form of three dots. Each subject was asked to declare whether the other three dots were moved by a real human (which happened to be yours truly, sitting quietly on the other side of the divider), or one of the two AI programs, which were sitting even more quietly inside of Bardia's laptop, waiting for his command to start.

Each subject was given about six to twelve tests, and was told to take as long as he or she needed to decide (we wanted to see if reaction time would be correlated with believability—it turns out that there was no correlation). Some subjects made their decisions within seconds (which were no more accurate than average) and some took longer, with a few going longer than a minute. Regarding the gesturing by the human subjects, some of them launched into bold symphonic gestures, while others timidly shifted their hands and head, barely creating any motion. Some subjects drew shapes in the air to get some visual language interaction going, and others just wobbled in place. Those subjects that displayed small, shy motions were met with equally shy AI behavior. The reason is that our AI algorithms were designed to detect a specific threshold of motion in the subjects, and these motions were not energetic enough to trigger a response. It was a bit like two shy people who are unable to get a conversation going.

Mirroring

As expected, most of the subjects could tell when the dots were being moved by the hidden human gesturer (me). Scientifically-speaking, it is a no-no for me to serve as the hidden human gesturer—as I am biased towards the results of the experiment (and I might be inclined to imitate the movements of one of my AI algorithms—possibly without even being aware of it) At any rate, I tried as best I could to just be myself: to look *human* (which was one of Turing's original rules).

Also as expected, the imitative AI algorithm scored better than the first one, in fooling the subjects into thinking it was human. But we were surprised by *how much* it fooled the subjects: almost half of them declared that it was human. And even more interesting is the fact none of the subjects made any comment suggesting that they were being aped.

An ape can tell that a reflected image in a mirror is not another ape, but is in fact the ape himself. Besides the great apes, only a few species have been identified as being able to pass the "mirror test" (including bottlenose dolphins and elephants). Our human ability for self-reflection is considerably more nuanced, automatic, and effortless. Mirroring is part of how we become acculturated. Mirror neurons are activated when we imitate each other, or when we witness another person having an experience that we have had. Mirror neurons are even activated when we *imagine* a person (or ourselves) having an experience. Our mirror neuron system is so eager and willing to do its job that we might be easily duped by even the simplest imitation.

Even though simple imitation in a virtual agent is effective, it can lose its effect over time once the human subject notices the slightest bit of unjustified repetition, or when it becomes apparent that there is actually no communicating going on—which is bound to happen eventually.

The Point

I had originally suggested that the Gestural Turing test be done with one single point (I love a challenge). It's hard to detect any indication of human anatomy from a single point. My hypothesis is this: given enough time to interact, two humans who want to convince each other

that they are alive will eventually succeed, even if all they have is a single point to move around. The existence of a human *mind* would eventually be revealed, and this would require a very human-like process of constructing, and then climbing, the semiotic ladder: spontaneously generating the visuo-dynamic symbols with which to communicate. Whether or not an AI can achieve this is another matter entirely. But in either case, I believe that the apprehension of a living other *could* be achieved using pure motion. This is the essence of the Gestural Turing Test, as well as the basis for designing motion algorithms that make virtual characters more believable.

Studying the essence of motion, and the intentions and emotions behind motions, doesn't just end with scientific (or pseudo-scientific) experimentation. It applies to the creation of social virtual worlds, the design of intuitive, conversational web interfaces that use natural affordances, and the art of procedural character animation—essentially, the applications of embodied AI. We have just drilled into the extreme distillation of expressive motion in the form of a terse alphabet so that we can have a foundation to explore some of the many ways that the apprehension and generation of living motion can play out in social media. We are now ready to explore the semiotics of tail wagging.

8

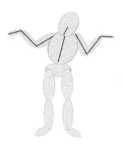

The Tail Wagging the Brain

The brain can rewire its neurons, growing new connections, well into old age. Marked recovery is often possible even in stroke victims, porn addicts, and obsessive-compulsive sufferers, several years after the onset of their conditions. *Neural Plasticity* is now proven to exist in adults, not just in babies and young children going through the critical learning stages of life. This subject has been popularized with books like *The Brain that Changes Itself* (Doidge 2007). Like language grammar, music theory, and dance, visual language can be developed throughout life. As visual stimuli are taken in repeatedly, our brains reinforce neural networks for recognizing and interpreting them. Some aspects of visual language are easily learned, and some may even be instinctual. *Biophilia* is the human aesthetic appreciation of biological form and all living systems (Kellert and Wilson 1993). The flip side of aesthetic biophilia is a readiness to learn disgust (of feces and certain smells) or fear (of large insects or snakes, for instance). Easy recognition of the shapes of branching trees, puffy clouds, flowing water, plump fruit, and subtle differences in the shades of green and red, have laid a foundation for human aesthetic response in all things, natural or manufactured. Our biophilia is the foundation of much of our visual design, even in areas as urban as abstract painting, web page layout, and office furniture design.

The Face

We all have visual language skills that make us especially sensitive to eyebrow motion, eye contact, head orientation, and mouth shape. Our sensitivity to facial expression may even influence other, more abstract forms of visual language, making us responsive to some visual signals more than others—because those face-specific sensitivities gave us an evolutionary advantage as a species so dependent on social signaling. This may have been reinforced by sexual selection. Even visual features as small as the pupil of an eye contribute to the emotional reading of a face—usually unconsciously. Perhaps the evolved sensitivity to small black dots as information-givers contributed to our subsequent invention of small-yet-critical elements in typographical alphabets.

We see faces in clouds, trees, and spaghetti. Donald Norman wrote a book called, *Turn Signals are the Facial Expressions of Automobiles* (1992). Recent studies using fMRI scans show that car aficionados use the same brain modules to recognize cars that people in general use to recognize faces (Gauthier et al. 2003). Something about the face appears to be baked into the brain.

Dog Smiling

We smile with our faces. Dogs smile with their tails. The next time you see a Doberman Pinscher with his ears clipped and his tail removed (docked), imagine yourself with your smile muscles frozen dead and your eyebrows shaved off.

Like humans perceiving human smiles, it is likely that the canine brain has neural wiring highly tuned to recognize and process a certain kind of visual energy: an oscillating motion of a linear shape occurring near the backside of another dog. The photoreceptors go to work doing edge detection and motion detection so they can send efficient signals to the brain for rapid space-time pattern recognition. Tail wagging is apparently a learned behavior: puppies don't wag until they are one or two months old. Recent findings in dog tail wagging show that a wagger will favor the right side as a result of feeling fundamentally positive about something, and will favor the left side when there are negative overtones in feeling (Quaranta et al. 2007). This is not something humans have commonly known until recently. Could it be that left-right wagging asymmetry has always been a subtle part of canine-to-canine body language?

I often watch intently as my terrier mix, Higgs, encounters a new dog in the park whom he has never met. The two dogs approach each other—often moving very slowly and cautiously. If the other dog has its tail down between its legs and its ears and head held down, and is frequently glancing to the side to avert eye contact, this generally means it is afraid, shy, or intimidated. If its tail is sticking straight up (and not wagging) and if its ears are perked up and the hair on the back is standing on end, it could mean trouble. But if the new stranger is wagging its tail, this is a pretty good sign that things are going to be just fine. Then a new phase of dog body language takes over. If Higgs is in a playful mood, he'll start a series of quick motions, squatting his chest down to assume the "play bow", jumping and stopping suddenly, and watching the other dog closely (probably to keep an eye on the tail, among other things). If Higgs is successful, the other dog will accept his invitation, and they will start running around the park, chasing each other, and having a grand old time. It is such a joy to watch dogs at play.

So here is a question: assuming dogs have an instinctive—or easily-learned—ability to process the body language of other dogs, like wagging tails, can the same occur in humans for processing canine body language? Did I have to learn to read canine body language from scratch, or was I was born with this ability? I am after all a member of a species that has been co-evolving with canines for more than ten thousand years, sometimes in deeply symbiotic relationships. So, perhaps I, Homo Sapiens, already have a biophilic predisposition to canine body language. Recent studies in using dogs as therapy for helping children with autism have shown remarkable results. These children become more socially and emotionally connected. According to autistic author Temple Grandin, this is because animals, like people with autism, do not experience ambivalent emotion; their emotions are pure and direct (Grandin, Johnson 2005). Perhaps canines helped to modulate, buffer, and filter human emotions throughout our symbiotic evolution. They may have helped to offset a tendency towards neurosis and cognitive chaos.

Vestigial Response

Having a dog in the family provides a continual reminder of my affiliation with canines, not just as companions, but as Earthly relatives. On a few rare occasions while sitting quietly at home working on something, I remember hearing an unfamiliar noise somewhere in the house. But before I even knew consciously that I was hearing anything, I felt a vague tug at my ears; it was not an entirely comfortable feeling. This may have happened at other times, but I probably didn't notice. I later learned that this is a leftover vestigial response that we inherited from our ancestors. The ability for some people to wiggle their ears is due to muscles that are basically useless in humans, but were once used by our ancestors to aim their ears toward a sound. Remembering the feeling of that tug on my ears gives me a feeling of connection to my ancestors' physical experiences.

In a moment we will consider how these primal vestiges might be coming back into modern currency. But I'm still in a meandering, storytelling, pipe-smoking kind of mood, so hang with me just a bit longer and then we'll get back to the subject of avatars.

This vestigial response is called *ear perking*. It is shared by many of our living mammalian relatives, including cats. I remember once hanging out and playing mind-games with a cat. I was sitting on a couch, and the cat was sitting in the middle of the floor, looking away, pretending to ignore me (but of course—it's a cat). I was trying to get the cat to look at me or to acknowledge me in some way. I called its name, I hissed, clicked my tongue, and clapped my hands. Nothing. I scratched the upholstery on the couch. Nothing. Then I tore a small piece of paper from my notebook, crumpled it into a tiny ball, and discreetly tossed it onto the floor, behind the cat, outside of its field of view. The tiny sound of the crumpled ball of paper falling to the floor caused one of the cat's ears to swivel around and aim towards the sound. I jumped up and yelled, "Hah—got you!" The cat's higher brain quickly tugged at its ear, pulling it back into place, and the cat continued to serenely look off into the distance, as if nothing had ever happened.

Cat body language is harder to read than dog body language. Perhaps that's by design (I mean...evolution). Dogs don't seem to have the same talents of reserve and constraint. Dog expressions just flop out in front of you. And their vocabulary is quite rich. Most world languages have several dog-related words and phrases. We easily learn to recognize the body language of dogs, and even less familiar social animals. Certain forms of body language are processed by the brain more easily than others. A baby learns to respond to its mother's smile very soon after birth. Learning to read a dog's tail motions may not be so instinctive, but the plastic brain of Homo Sapiens is ready to adapt. Learning to read the signs that your pet turtle is hungry would be much harder (I assume). At the extreme: learning to read the signals from an enemy character in a complicated computer game may be a skill only for a select few elite players.

This I'm sure of: if we had tails, we'd be wagging them for our dogs when they are being good (and for that matter, we'd also be wagging them for each other :D). It would not be easy to add a tail to the base of a human spine and wire up the nerves and muscles. But if it could be done, our brains would easily and happily adapt, employing some appropriate system of neurons to the purpose of wagging the tail—perhaps re-adapting a system of neurons normally dedicated to doing *The Twist*. While it may not be easy to adapt our bodies to acquire such organs of expression, our brains can easily adapt. And that's where avatars come in.

Furries

The Furry Species has proliferated in Second Life. Furry Fandom is a subculture featuring fictional anthropomorphic animal characters with human personalities and human-like attributes. Furry fandom already had a virtual head start—people were role-playing with their online "fursonas" before Second Life existed (witness FurryMUCK, a user-extendable online text-based role-playing game started in 1990). Furries have animal heads, tails, and other such features.

(Image: Francis 7)

While many Second Life avatars have true animal forms (such as the "ferals" and the "tinies"), many are anthropomorphic: walking upright with human postures and gaits. This anthropomorphism has many creative expressions, ranging from quaint and cute to mythical, scary, and kinky.

Furry anthropomorphism in Second Life is appropriate in one sense: there is no way to directly change the Second Life avatar into a non-human form. The underlying avatar skeleton software is based solely on the upright-walking human form. I know this fact in an intimate way, because I spent several months digging into the code in an attempt to reconstitute the avatar skeleton to allow open-ended morphologies (quadrupeds, etc.) This proved to be difficult. And no surprise: the humanoid avatar morphology code, and all its associated animations—procedural and otherwise—had been in place for several years. It serves a similar purpose to a group of genes in our DNA called *Hox genes*. They are baked deep into our genetic structure, and are critical to the formation of a body plan. Hox genes specify the overall structure of the body and are critical in embryonic development when the segmentation and placement of limbs and other body parts are first established. After struggling to override the effects of the Second Life "avatar Hox genes", I concluded that I could not do this on my own. It was a strategic surgical process that many core Linden Lab engineers would have to perform. Evolution in virtual worlds happens fast. It's hard to go back to an earlier stage and start over.

Despite the anthropomorphism of the Second Life avatar (or perhaps *because* of this constraint), the Linden scripting language (LSL) and other customizing abilities have provided a means for some remarkably creative workarounds, including packing the avatar geometry into a small compact form called a "meatball", and then surrounding it with a custom 3D object, such as a robot or a dragon or some abstract form, complete with responsive animations and particle system effects.

Perhaps furry residents prefer having this constraint of anthropomorphism; it fits with their nature as *hybrids*. Some furry residents have customized tail animations and use them to express mood and intent. I wouldn't be surprised if those who have been furries for many years have dreams in which they are living and expressing in their Furry bodies—communicating with tails, ears, and all. Most would agree that customizing a Furry with a wagging-tail animation is a lot easier than undergoing surgery to attach a physical tail. But as far as the brain is concerned, it may not make a difference.

Where Does my Virtual Body Live?

Virtual reality is not manifest in computer chips, computer screens, headsets, keyboards, mice, joysticks, or head-mounted displays. Nor does it live in running software. Virtual reality manifests in the brain, and in the collective brains of societies. The blurring of real and virtual experiences is a theme that Jeremy Bailenson and his team at Stanford's Virtual Human Interaction Lab have been researching. Virtual environments are now being used for research in social sciences, as well as for the treatment of many brain disorders. An amputee who has suffered from phantom pain for years can be cured of the pain through a disciplined and focused regimen of rewiring his or her body image to effectively "amputate" the phantom limb. Immersive virtual reality has been used recently to treat this problem (Murray et al. 2007). Previous techniques using physical mirrors have been replaced with sophisticated simulations that allow more controlled settings and adjustments. When the brain's body image gets tweaked away from reality too far, psychological problems ensue, such as anorexia. Having so many super-thin sex-symbol avatars may not be helping the situation. On the other hand, virtual reality is being used in research to treat this and other body image-related disorders.

A creative kind of short-term body image shifting is nothing new to animators, actors, and puppeteers, who routinely tweak their own body images in order to express like ostriches or hummingbirds or dogs. When I was working for Brad deGraf, one of the early pioneers in real-time character animation, I would frequent the offices of Protozoa, a game company he founded in the mid-90s. I was hired to develop a tool for modeling 3D trees which were to be used in a game called "Squeezils", featuring animals that scurry among the branches. I remember the first time I went to Protozoa. I was waiting in the lobby to meet Brad, and I noticed a video monitor at the other end of the room. An animation was playing that had a couple of 3D characters milling about. One of them was a crab-like cartoon character with huge claws, and the other was a Big Bird-like character with a very long neck. After gazing at these characters for a while, it occurred to me that both of these characters were moving in coordination—as if they were both being puppeteered by the same person. My curiosity got the best of me and I started wandering around the offices, looking for the puppet master. I peeked around the corner. In the next room were a couple of motion capture experts, testing their hardware. On the stage was a guy wearing motion capture gear. When his arms moved, so did the huge claws of the crab—and so did the wimpy wings of the tall bird. When his head moved, the eyes of the crab looked around, and the bird's head moved around on top of its long neck.

Brad deGraf and puppeteer/animator Emre Yilmaz call this "…performance animation…a new kind of jazz. Also known as digital puppetry…it brings characters to life, i.e. 'animates' them, through real-time control of the three-dimensional computer renderings, enabled by fast graphics computers, live motion sampling, and smart software" (deGraf and Yilmaz 1999). When applying human-sourced motion to exaggerated cartoon forms, the human imagination is stimulated: "motion capture" escapes its negative association with droll, unimaginative literal recording. It inspires the human controller to think more like a puppeteer than an actor. Puppeteering is more *out-of-body* than acting. Anything can become a puppet (a sock, a salt shaker, a rubber hose).

(Image: Ventrella)

deGraf and Yilmaz make this out-of-body transference possible by "re-proportioning" the data stream from the human controller to fit non-human anatomies.

Non-human puppeteered characters (Image: Brad deGraf, Dan Hanna, and Emre Yilmaz)

Research by Nick Yee found that people's behaviors change as a result of having different virtual representations, a phenomenon he calls the *Proteus Effect* (Yee 2007). Artist Micha Cardenas spent 365 hours continuously as a dragon in Second Life. She employed a Vicon motion capture system to translate her motions into the virtual world. This project, called "Becoming Dragon", explored the limits of body modification, "challenging" the one-year transition requirement that

148

transgender people face before gender confirmation surgery. Cardenas told me, "The dragon as a figure of the shapeshifter was important to me to help consider the idea of permanent transition, rejecting any simple conception of identity as tied to a single body at a single moment, and instead reflecting on the process of learning a new way of moving, walking, talking and how that breaks down any possible concept of an original or natural state for the body to be in" (Cardenas 2010).

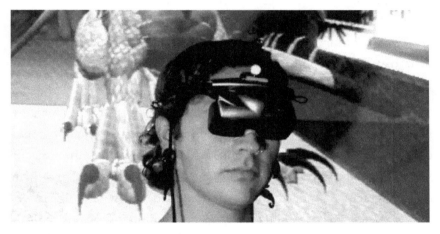

Micha Cardenas became a dragon avatar for 365 hours straight (Image: Cardenas)

With this performance, Cardenas wanted to explore not only the issues surrounding gender transformation, but the larger question of how we experience our bodies, and what it means to inhabit the body of another being—real or simulated. During this 365-hour art-performance, the lines between real and virtual progressively blurred for Cardenas, and she found herself "thinking" in the body of a dragon. What interests me is this: how did Micha's brain adapt to be able to "think" in a different body? What happened to her *body image*?

The Homunculus

Dr. Wilder Penfield was operating on a patient's brain to relieve symptoms of epilepsy. In the process he made a remarkable discovery: each part of the body is associated with a specific region in the brain. He had discovered the *homunculus*: a map of the body in the brain. The homunculus is an invisible cartoon character. It can only be "seen" by carefully probing parts of it and asking the patient what he or she is feeling, or by watching different parts of the body twitch in response. Most interesting is the fact that some parts of the homunculus are much larger than others—totally out of proportion with normal human anatomy. There are two primary "homunculi" (sensory and motor) and their distorted proportions correspond to the relative differences in how much of the brain is dedicated to the different regions.

For instance, eyes, lips, tongue, and hands are proportionately large, whereas the skull and thighs are proportionately small. I would not want to encounter a homunculus while walking down the street or hanging out at a party—homunculi are not pretty—in fact, I find them quite frightening. Indeed they have cropped up in haunting ways throughout the history of literature, science, and philosophy.

But happily, for purposes of my research, any homunculus I encounter would be very good at nonverbal communication, because eyes, mouth, and hands are major expressive organs of the body. As a general rule, the parts of our body that receive the most information are also the parts that give the most. What would a "concert pianist homunculus" look like? Huge fingers. How about a "soccer player homunculus"? Gargantuan legs and tiny arms.

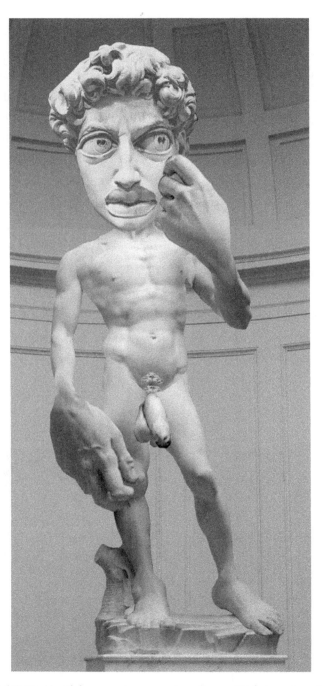

Michelangelo's *David* with homuncular proportions (Image: Michelangelo and Ventrella)

The Homuncular Avatar

Avatar code etches embodiment into virtual space. A "communication homunculus" was sitting on my shoulder while I was working at There.com and arguing with some computer graphics guys about how to engineer the avatar. Chuck Clanton and I were both advocates for dedicating more polygons and procedural animation capability to the avatar's hands and face. But polygons are graphics-intensive (at least they were back then), and procedural animation takes a lot of engineering work. Consider this: in order to properly animate two articulated avatar hands, you need at least twenty extra joints, on top of the approximately twenty joints used in a typical avatar animation skeleton. That's nearly twice as many joints.

The argument for full hand articulation was as follows: like the proportions of cortex dedicated to these communication-intensive areas of the body, socially-oriented avatars should have ample resources dedicated to face and hands.

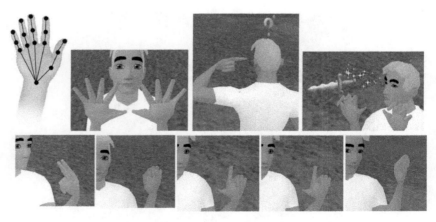

A prototype of hand articulation and animation for There.com (Image: Ventrella)

When the developers of Traveler were faced with the problem of how to squeeze the most out of the few polygons they could render on the screen at any given time, they decided to just make avatars as floating heads—because their world centered on vocal communication (telephone meets avatar). The developers of ActiveWorlds, which had a similar polygonal predicament, chose whole avatar bodies (and they were quite clunky by today's standards).

These kinds of choices determine where and how human expression will manifest.

Non-Human Avatars

Avatar body language does not have to be a direct prosthetic to our corporeal expression. It can extend beyond the human form; this theme has been a part of avatar lore since the very beginning. What are the implications for a non-human body language alphabet? It means that our body language alphabet can (and I would claim already has begun to) include semantic units, attributes, descriptors, and grammars that encompass a superset of human form and behavior.

The illustration below shows pentadactl morphology of various vertebrate limbs. This has implications for a common underlying code used to express meta-human forms and motions.

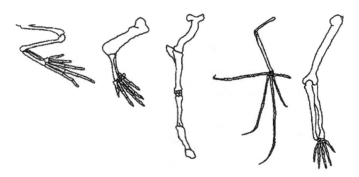

Comparative anatomy of animal limbs

A set of parameters (bone lengths, angle offsets, motor control attributes, etc.) can be specified, along with gross morphological settings (i.e., four limbs and a tail; six limbs and no head; no limbs and no head, etc.) Once these parameters are provided in the system to accommodate the various locomotion behaviors and forms of body language, they can be manipulated as *genes*, using interactive evolution interfaces or genetic algorithms, or simply tweaked directly in a customization interface.

But this morphological space of variation doesn't need to stop at the vertebrates. We've seen avatars in the form of fishes, floating eyeballs, cartoon characters, abstract designs—you name it. Artists, in the spirit of performance artist Stelarc, are exploring the expressive possibilities of avatars and remote embodiment. Micha Cardenas, Max Moswitzer, Jeremy Owen Turner and others articulate the very aesthetics of embodiment and avatarhood—the entire possible expression-space. What are the possibilities of having a visual (or even aural) manifestation of yourself in an alternate reality? As I mentioned before, my Second Life avatar is a non-humanoid creature, consisting of a cube with tentacles.

The author's Second Life avatar with JoannaTrail Blazer (Image: Joanna Trailblazer)

On each side of the cube are fractals based on an image of my face. This cube floats in space where my head would normally be. Attached to the bottom of the cube are several green tentacles that hang like those of a jellyfish. This avatar was built by JoannaTrail Blazer, based on my design. In the illustration, Joanna's avatar is shown next to mine.

I chose a non-human form for a few reasons: One reason is that I prefer to avoid the uncanny valley, and will go to extremes in avoiding droll realism, employing instead the visual tools of abstraction and symbolism. By not trying to replicate the image of a real human, I can sidestep the problem of my avatar "not looking like me" or "not looking right". My non-human avatar also allows me to explore the realm of non-human body language. On the one hand, I can express yes and no by triggering animations that cause the cube to oscillate like a normal head. But I could also express happiness or excitement by triggering an animation that causes the tentacles to flair out and oscillate, or to roll sensually like an inverted bouquet of cat tails. Negative emotions could be represented by causing the tentacles to droop limply (reinforced by having the cube-head slump downward). While the cube-head mimics normal human head motions, the tentacles do not correspond to any body language that I am physically capable of generating. They could tap other sources, like animal movement, and basic concepts like energy and gravity, expanding my capacity for expression.

Virtual Dogs

I want to come back to the topic of canine body language now, but this time, I'd like to discuss some of the ways that sheer dogginess in the gestalt can be expressed in games and virtual worlds. The canine species has made many appearances throughout the

history of animation research, games, and virtual worlds. Rob Fulop, of the '90s game company PF Magic, created a series of games based on characters made of spheres, including the game "Dogz". Bruce Blumberg of the MIT Media Lab developed a virtual interactive dog AI, and is also an active dog trainer. Dogs are a great subject for doing AI—they are easier to simulate than humans, and they are highly emotional, interactive, and engaging.

While prototyping There.com, Will and I developed a dog that would chase a virtual Frisbee tossed by your avatar (involving simultaneous mouse motion to throw the Frisbee and hitting the space key to release the Frisbee at the right time). Since I was interested in the "essence of dog energy", I decided not to focus on the graphical representation of the dog so much as the motion, sound, and overall behavior of the dog. So, for this prototype, the dog had no legs: just a sphere for a body and a sphere for a head (each rendered as toon-shaded circles—flat coloring with an outline). These spheres could move slightly relative to each other, so that the head had a little bounce to it when the dog jumped.

The eyes were rendered as two black cartoon dots, and they would disappear when the dog blinked. Two ears, a tail, and a tongue were programmed, because they are expressive components. The ears were animated using forward dynamics, so they flopped around when the dog moved, and hung downward slightly from the force of gravity. I programmed some simple logic to make an oscillating, "panting" force in the tongue which would increase in frequency and force when the dog was especially active, tired, or nervous. I also programmed "ear perkiness" which would cause the ears to aim upwards (still with a little bit of droop) whenever a nearby avatar produced a chat that included the dog's name. I programmed the dog to change its mood when a nearby avatar produced the chats "good dog" or "bad dog". And this was just the beginning. Later, I added more AI allowing the dog to learn to recognize chat words, and to bond to certain avatars.

Despite the lack of legs and its utterly crude rendering, this dog elicited remarkable puppy-like responses in the people who watched it or played with it. The implication from this is that what makes a dog a dog is not merely the way it looks, but the way it acts— its essence as a distinctly canine space-time energy event. Recall the exaggerated proportions of the human *communication homunculus*. For this dog, ears, tail, and tongue constituted the vast majority of computational processing. That was on purpose; this dog was intended as a communicator above all else. Consider the visual language of tail wagging that I brought up earlier, a visual language which humans (especially dog-owners) have incorporated into their unconscious vocabularies. What lessons might we take from the subject of *wag semiotics*, as applied to the art and science of wagging on the internet?

Tail Wagging on the Internet

In the There.com dog, the tail was used as a critical indicator of its mood at any given moment, raising when the dog was alert or aroused, drooping when sad or afraid, and wagging when happy. Take wagging as an example. The body language information packet for tail wagging consisted of a Boolean value sent from the dog's Brain to the dog's Animated Body, representing simply "start wagging" or "stop wagging". It is important to note that the dog's Animated Body is constituted on clients (computers sitting in front of users), whereas the dog's Brain resides on servers (arrays of big honkin' computers in a data center that manage the "shared reality" of all users). The reason for this mind/body separation is to make sure that body language messaging (as well as overall emotional state, physical location and orientation of the dog, and other aspects of its dynamic state) are truthfully conveyed to all the users.

Clients are subject to animation frame rates lagging, internet messages dropping out, and other issues. All users whose avatars are hanging out in a part of the virtual world where the dog is hanging out need to see the same behavior; they are all "seeing the same dog"— virtually-speaking.

Dogs in There.com (images: There.com)

It would be unnecessary (and expensive in terms of internet traffic) for the server to send individual wags several times a second to all the clients. Each client's Animated Body code is perfectly capable of performing this repetitive animation. And, because of different rendering speeds among various clients, lag times, etc, the wagging tail on *your* client might be moving left-right-left-right, while the wagging tail on my client is moving right-left-right-left. In other words, they might be out of phase or wagging at slightly different speeds. These slight differences have almost no effect on the reading of the wag. "I am wagging my tail" is the point. That's a Boolean message: one bit. The reason I am laboring over this point harkens back to the chapter on a Body Language Alphabet: a data-compressed message, easy to zip through the internet, is efficient for helping virtual worlds run smoothly. It is also inspired by biosemiotics: Mother Nature's efficient message-passing protocol.

On Cuttlefish and Dolphins

The homunculus of Homo Sapiens might evolve into a more plastic form—maybe not on a genetic/species level, but at least during the lifetimes of individual brains, assisted by the scaffolding of culture and virtual world technology. This plasticity could approach strange proportions, even as our physical bodies remain roughly the same. As we spend more of our time socializing and interacting on the internet as part of the program to travel less to reduce greenhouse gases, our embodiment will naturally take on the forms appropriate to the virtual spaces we occupy. And these spaces will not necessarily mimic the spaces of the real world, nor will our embodiments always look and feel like our own bodies. And with these new virtual embodiments will come new layers of body language. Jaron Lanier uses the example of cephalopods as species capable of animated texturemapping and physical morphing used for communication and camouflage—feats that are outside the range of physical human expression.

In reference to avatars, Lanier says, "The problem is that in order to morph, humans must design avatars in laborious detail in advance. Our software tools are not yet flexible enough to enable us, in virtual reality, to think ourselves into different forms. Why would we want to? Consider the existing benefits of our ability to create sounds with our mouths. We can make new noises and mimic existing ones, spontaneously and instantaneously. But when it comes to visual communication, we are hamstrung…We can learn to draw and paint,

159

or use computer-graphics design software. But we cannot generate images at the speed with which we can imagine them" (Lanier 2006).

Cuttlefish body language includes animated skin

Once we have developed the various non-humanoid puppeteering interfaces that would allow Lanier's vision, we will begin to invent new visual languages for realtime communication. Lanier believes that in the future, humans will be truly "multihomuncular".

Researchers from Aberdeen University and the Polytechnic University of Catalonia found that dolphins use discrete units of body language as they swim together near the surface of water. They observed efficiency in these signals, similar to what occurs in frequently-used words in human verbal language (Ferrer i Cancho and Lusseau 2009). As human natural language goes online, and as our body language gets processed, data-compressed, and alphabetized for efficient traversal over the internet, we may start to see more patterns of our embodied language that resemble those created by dolphins, and many other social species besides. The background communicative buzz of the biosphere may start to make more sense in the process of whittling our own communicative energy down to its essential features, and being able to analyze it digitally. With a universal body language alphabet, we might someday be able to animate our skin like cephalopods, or speak "dolphin", using our tails, as we lope across the virtual waves.

9

Verbal Ectoplasm

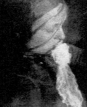

When I was young I used to sneak into my brother's bedroom and look at his paperback books. Mike had quite a collection: science fiction, politics, humor, and, strangely, a collection of books about the paranormal. This last category of books was especially intriguing to me. I remember thumbing through the pages and seeing odd black-and-white pictures of people accompanied by half-faded ghostly shapes with faces in them. These ghostly shapes, presumably captured in photographs, were referred to as "ectoplasm". Sometimes this stuff would be oozing from various orifices: mouths, ears, noses, etc. Ectoplasm is the stuff that ghosts are made of—spiritual energy manifested physically—so we mortals can experience it.

Chat balloons are noncreepy ectoplasm, emitted from avatar mouths (or heads) when their users speak (or think). Chat balloons manifest the energy of verbal communication in physical blobs that rise above avatar heads and float in space. They provide an embodiment of

texts so that they can take up
residence with the other embodied
communicative agents in the virtual
world (like faces, bodies, clothes, and
props). Thus, chat balloons can be
used to creatively express nonverbal

concepts that would be impossible to express with words alone.

Chat balloons that bubble up in virtual worlds are evoked from
our world (a higher world). We, the higher beings, speak through these
ectoplasmic inpourings. This is not unlike the original notion of
"avatar" itself (Sanskrit for "descent"), whereby a higher being
descends into the mortal world.

Chat balloons in virtual worlds are evoked from a higher realm (Image: Ventrella)

In virtual worlds, chat balloons allow words to get dressed up
in body language, by virtue of their having nonverbal (i.e., visuo-
dynamic) attributes. As embodied nonverbal communication, chat
balloons can express many levels of meaning and affect. We've seen it

in comic books, when the voice from a telephone, for instance, creates a different kind of balloon tail, or when a dominant character's balloons crowd out those of other characters. Early versions of chat balloons were introduced in virtual worlds such as *Habitat*, *Worlds Away*, and *Alphaworld*. In *The Palace*, users could emit different styles of chat balloons, as shown here.

The Palace: an early example of chat balloon body language in virtual worlds

Chat balloons can contain visual symbols as well.

Chat balloon cartoons by the author (Image: Ventrella)

The characters in *The Sims* produce pictorial *thought bubbles* while generating audible gibberish ("Simlish"), showing what they are thinking or what they want. By introducing text (and pictorial utterings) into the 3D scene, chat balloons also serve another goal: they put verbal communication in closer visual proximity to the locus of natural language—the *body*. This helps reduce the distance the eye has to jump in order to take in both verbal and nonverbal language. The user's text floats above the avatars, connected to the 3D environment. This keeps the user's eyes from having to make big jumps between text land and avatar land.

A Sims character making a thought bubble (image: Electronic Arts)

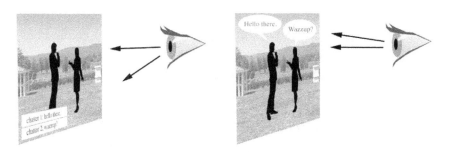

Chat balloons allow verbal language to appear closer to the "source" (Image: Ventrella)

Managing Balloon Hell

When there are only a few characters in a 2D side-scrolling scene, chat balloon layout is relatively manageable, as was done in Microsoft's Comic Chat (Kurlander et al. 1996). In Comic Chat, users could customize certain aspects of a graphical chat experience.

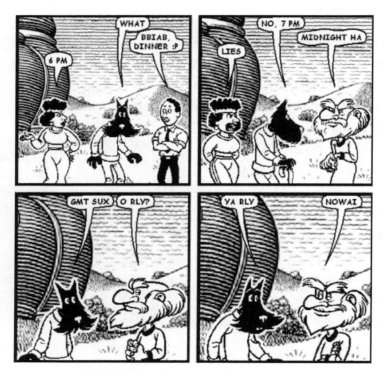

Microsoft Comic Chat 2.5 (image from Wikipedia, December 2010)

While the participants engaged in conversation, comic book-like features were automated, including the generation of new comic panels when chat balloons fill up the space.

In the case of 3D virtual worlds where numerous avatars might be milling about randomly and producing a cacophony of chat balloons, things can get messy pretty quickly. This is illustrated on the next page with two screenshots: one of the game, *Pirates of the Burning Sea*, and the other of Second Life (with the chat bubble feature turned on).

Chat Balloon Hell in *Pirates of the Burning Sea*

Chat Balloon Hell in *Second Life* (Image: Ventrella)

167

How can the chat balloons in such a situation be rallied into good behavior? The techniques that we developed at There.com were designed specifically to overcome these problems—although they were far from perfect. Our technique can be explained with two rather cute metaphors: helium-filled balloons, and a water wheel rotating in reverse. The helium-filled balloons represent the horizontal arrangement of chat balloons, and the water wheel represents their vertical arrangement.

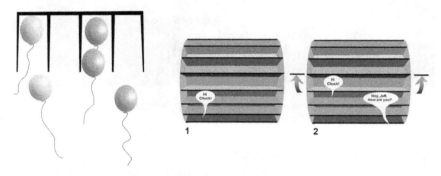

Metaphors for organizing chat balloons to facilitate conversational dynamics (Image: Ventrella)

Remember chapter Four where I described the design of Avatar-Centric Communication? When users move their avatars together to form a cluster and start generating text, a *Chat Group* is automatically formed—visualized in the prototype as a hula hoop surrounding the group. This feature was later replaced with manual triggers for starting chat groups. The intentional formation of a chat group causes the avatars' chat balloons to organize themselves in a more orderly way. They take positions in evenly-spaced columns, and line up above their heads, beneath their nametags, as shown on the next page. The chronology of the conversation is visualized by the vertical placement of the chat balloons. As a new chat balloon is emitted, an invisible "inverse water wheel" rotates by one notch, holding the chat balloons within its tidy paddles, causing all the balloons to rise up at an even rate. Older (higher) chat balloons float out of view at the top of the screen, while fresh new chats appear above the avatars' heads.

Example of four chat balloon registers in a chat group (Image: There.com)

The illustration on the next page shows how vertical positioning of chat balloons helps to separate parts of the conversation in time, made possible by the ability to see balloons filling up with words (as explained later).

Balloons fill up with words in realtime (Image: Ventrella)

This vertical arrangement also provides the means for a number of possible interactions by which users can refer to earlier parts of the conversations, as shown below.

The user selects an earlier balloon to respond to that text (Image: Ventrella)

In this example the user, whose avatar is in the middle, has selected one of the chat balloons on the right, thereby indicating that he/she is responding to the chat in that balloon, rather than the last one the user generated.

Attenuated Chatter in the Distance

The chat balloon serves as a visual metaphor for acoustic sound (only it persists for a longer period—so perhaps it might be better to describe it as a metaphor for recent memory of spoken words). Like sound, chat balloons can *attenuate* with distance; their appearance in the user's field of view can shrink and become translucent, like a distant murmur.

Thanks to what is called *the cocktail party effect*, our brains are able to tune-out chatter in the distance (and periphery) while attention is focused on a conversation with one person, standing out among the aural clutter. In the same spirit, a chat balloon scheme was designed for There.com that distinguishes high-priority chat balloons from low-priortity ones. In the illustration on the next page we see a transluscent panel floating off to the left. This represents my camera view onto a group of avatars (which includes *my* avatar) as I would see it on my computer screen. Off to the right we see a distant group of avatars chatting away. They are generating *low-priority* chat balloons. Low-priority chat balloons are smaller and transluscent, and they can overlap each other, which makes them not always legible. Although they are not always legible, low-priority chat baloons do reveal aspects of the dynamics of the conversation. Frequency of balloon generation can show how much talking is going on. It is also apparent when one avatar is doing most of the talking.

My chat group (left) and a distant chat group (right)

An avatar leaves the distant chat group to join mine

The avatar joins my chat group (images: Ventrella)

In the three previous illustrations, an avatar leaves the distant chat group and joins my chat group. As soon as she joins, her chat balloon becomes high-priority and gets incorporated into the balloon arrangement of my chat group—a new column is formed, and the other balloons shift to make room.

Interweaving Nonverbal Expression with Text

With standard instant messaging, a user's text is sent over the wires of the internet only after he/she hits the enter key (carriage return) on the keyboard or hits the send button. Earlier I spoke of the "collision" of text chat (occupying typographic space) with 3D animated avatars, describing them as *strange bedfellows*. One of the many quirky side effects of this collision is the fact that text gets sent infrequently, in isolated chunks, while the avatar (and any emotive animations it may be playing) is streaming its expression in realtime. This is not what happens in real life; a momentary raised eyebrow or a tiny smirk often accompanies the initial utterance of a word, providing meaning and nuance simultaneous to the verbal channel. In natural language, gesture and word are inseparable—two facets of a single communicative energy flow.

Bob Moore, a researcher at Yahoo! Labs who studies social interaction in online and offline environments, observes: "Speaking-by-typing is hidden from public view, with utterances emerging fully formed. The interactional result is that one's friend will walk away while one is still speaking, or one's teammate will attack when one is still discussing tactics" (2009).

For this reason, Chuck Clanton and I designed a feature of the avatar chat system that allows gestures to occur along with the words that are being generated. This was done using what we called "word-at-a-time" chat. As the user enters text, the individual words get sent over the internet as soon as a space character, period, or other terminating character is typed. As the words accumulate in the balloon, it expands as it fills-up, and when it reaches a certain limit, it breaks off and rises, leaving room for another balloon below to start filling with new words. Word-at-a-time chat allows the user the option to insert avatar facial expressions and gestures in-between the words being generated. We decided that the generation of one's verbal ectoplasm should not delay that person's ability to generate visual expressions. You wouldn't want that, would you? This is why word-at-a-time was invented.

To explain how word-at-a-time chat works, two variations of a user creating text and making associated avatar expressions are described below. Example 1 shows what happens using the standard text chat system, followed by triggering a nonverbal expression. Example 2 shows the exact same text but with multiple nonverbal expressions inserted between words.

Example 1:

1.   **User enters text: "Hi Betty. Nice to see you! Hey...what's wrong?"**

2.   **User hits carriage return (to send the text)**

3.   **User triggers *concerned* avatar expression**

Example 2:

1.   **User enters text: "Hi Betty."**

2.   **User triggers avatar *wave***

3.   **User adds text: "Nice to see you!"**

4.   **User triggers avatar *smile***

5.   **User adds text: "Hey..."**

6.   **User triggers *concerned* avatar expression**

7.   **User adds text: "what's wrong?"**

8.   **User hits carriage return (to finish filling up the chat balloon)**

The Ballooning of Chat

I have described just a few of the many tricks and techniques that allow text chat to be embodied in a virtual world, computer game, or user interface. Chat balloons have a long history. And they are alive and well, thriving in many media forms, including in mobile devices used for texting, to denote attributes of a conversation. In virtual world design, chat balloons are stirred around in a postmodern broth along with cinema, computer simulation, and other  ingredients. Chat balloons are a form of embodied communication—a visual representation of speech with a connection to a source (the tail). As a form of animated visual language, they are capable of an infinite range of expression. I can only expect chat balloons to continue evolving and popping up in user interfaces more and more.

A chat balloon can store conversational topics for later reference (Image: Ventrella)

Chat balloons visualize the occurrence of verbal communication in simulated space, and they make it clear *who* is talking. But they are not capable of indicating *who* is being *talked to*. *That* is most easily indicated by eye contact. In the next chapter, we will look at this powerful channel of communication. Like the visualization of chat balloons I have just shown you, I will apply visual overlays to social gaze, to demonstrate how complex and dynamic eye contact can be.

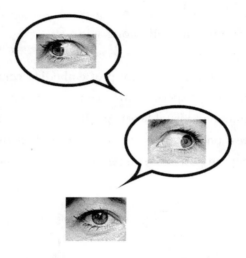

10

The Three-Dimensional Music of Gaze

Welcome to my laboratory! I would like to show you a device I invented that reveals an important property of social signaling. It visualizes 3D rays corresponding to what people are looking at. These rays originate from their eyes and land on what they are focusing on. In order to see these rays, you have to wear a HUD (Heads Up Display). I call it my "Gaze Vector HUD". I have uploaded the data visualization software onto two HUDS: one for you and one for me. I suggest we go to a nightclub so you can see how it works. At the nightclub, most of the people will be busy looking each other up and down. Gaze body language is generally cranked up to full blast at a nightclub. Don't worry, they look just like normal nerdy glasses, so no one will notice. We may have to dance a bit in order to not be too obvious.

I tried it out recently while walking down the street. I could see exactly where everyone was looking. The effect is a bit like kinetic abstract art, or visual jazz—white laser beams shooting in all directions, but not randomly; there is a rhythm to these beams. My algorithm lets me eavesdrop (or should I say, "eyesdrop") on people, to see where they are looking. To show the amazing variety of directed gaze, here are some screenshots taken from my gaze vector HUD :

Screenshots from the "gaze vector HUD" showing direction of gaze (images: Ventrella)

These screenshots can't capture the true dynamics of what's going on. You know the old saying: A picture is worth a thousand words. Well, an *animation* is worth a *thousand pictures*. Let me give you an example of what these image are not able to show you. I was in a coffee shop, wearing my Gaze Vector HUD, and watching a young man *pretend* he was reading a novel. It was obvious to me that Dostoyevsky was not on his mind: there were no indications of scanning within the book's pages, and his frequent glances up at the young lady with the mocha latte were frequent and well-timed (when she was looking the other way). I saw another fellow sitting off to the side who seemed to be looking at the floor tiling most of the time. In fact, it almost appeared as if he were coming up with mathematical equations based on the tile patterns, judging by the way his gaze vector would jump around in regular fashion and then occasionally stop.

Below are a few more screenshots. At the left is a screenshot of a young girl with her dog, sitting outside a grocery store (the girl was looking at the sidewalk when I grabbed this image, and the dog was fixated on the door of the grocery store). At the right is a screenshot of some people in an art gallery. Two of the people are looking up at the ceiling (the woman in the foreground is looking at the man who is looking up).

More screenshots from the gaze vector HUD (Image: Ventrella)

When two people are looking at each other, their gaze vectors become fused:

The gaze vector HUD reveals mutual eye contact (Image: Ventrella)

What I'm discovering with my gaze vector HUD is that there is a complex patterning to social gaze. It happens in 3D, and it changes constantly. I wore my gaze vector HUD in a company meeting recently (I told my colleagues that they were prescription glasses that I had to wear just for one day). At this meeting, the manager of the team was discussing our project. His gaze vector was dashing between all the people in the room; he seemed to be able to catch the eyes of everyone. That's a great skill to have if you want to build rapport—I wish I could be as good at it as he is! At meetings, I'm so consumed by the motions of people's hands and eyebrows, I often miss what's being said. Anyway, since there were about twelve people in the room, the manager had to zap his beams quite rapidly around the room in order to get everyone's eyes as he spoke. Quite impressive to see his technique in action.

By the way, in case you suspect that I am kidding about my "ingenious" gaze vector HUD, you are right. If you thought this device was real...sorry to disappoint you. But hey, if I could invent it...I surely would! Because it's really the way I look at the world—or rather, it's the way I look at how other people look at the world.

I have always wondered how people are able to switch their gaze so fast—we are, after all, analog machines—animals with parts made of flesh, bones, blood vessels and nerves. I read up on eyeball physiology and found out that eyes create the fastest movement in the human body. The rotational velocity of oculomotor movement can reach a thousand degrees a second. The human head rotates much slower than the eyeballs—not surprisingly: it's a lot heavier than an eyeball, and it contains two of them. Eyeballs constitute a small proportion of the mass of the head, which is so massive because it also contains a huge lump of fat called the brain and the cranium that protects it. I suppose it was more optimal for the oculomotor system to evolve for rapidly taking in the environment, instead of head movement, as the human brain grew in size during the course of evolution.

The speed of eye movement allows for the quick "once over", scanning from the top of an attractive prospect down the body and back up—sometimes happening in a tiny fraction of a second. I once saw this happen at Turk's Café: a young woman put her index finger on her partner's chest, smiled, and evoked a quick once-over to his chest and back up again. If I had blinked I would have missed it. But I'm glad I caught it. I wondered if she was an actress who knew exactly how to generate such subtle body language. On the other hand, she might have been too uncontrollably smitten to accomplish this on her own. Maybe Cupid had stepped into her body and was doing the puppeteering.

Saccades

The rapid changes in eye gaze are called *saccadic* eye movement, or simply, *saccades*. As the eyes take snapshots of the environment, the brain builds a stable model of the environment, even as the images landing on the retina are jumping around like a wild music video.

Eye-tracking instrumentation has been used to measure the saccades of viewers when looking at images. The illustration below shows how a viewer's focus jumps around on a face, typically spending more time on the eyes.

When viewing an image of a face, the focus jumps around in saccades (Image: Botticelli and Ventrella)

Many birds don't have the same eye-orbiting talents that we have, and so they have to use their heads to take these snapshots for visual fixation—a behavior called "head bobbing". These bird-saccades are timed with their struts, famously demonstrated by chickens and enthusiastic funk musicians. This strut allows the bird's head to be stationary for a brief moment between thrusts, so that the brain can take a picture. It's not unlike *spotting*: the head-shifting technique used by ballet dancers when they are rapidly spinning in place.

Saccade as Sign

For our purposes, what is interesting about saccadic behavior is not just its utility for taking in reality, but how this behavior is a part of natural language. It's not just used for input; it is used for output as well. The eyes of many social mammals have evolved distinct visual features—with clarity and utility reaching a high level in humans.

Image: Ventrella

The stark contrast between the iris and the whites of the eyes, the use of eye-widening to expose this contrast, and the distinct line of the eyebrow with its quick mobility—these can be explained as the evolutionary by-product of a highly communicative species.

Saccades evolved for building stable models of the world via snapshots. Saccades are important for us primates: since we have high foveal acuity (a high density of photoreceptor cells in the region of the fovea) we aim precisely at points in the environment to resolve details. But the evolution of saccades might have been intertwined with social adaptation as well. This behavior may have evolved not only for taking-in information from the environment, but also for sending messages out to the environment. Consider the following sentence that you might read in a novel: "Immediately after Mary told Bob what had happened, she made a split-second glance over to Frank—silently alluding to his involvement". (A plug for my imaginary Gaze Vector HUD: the algorithm runs at 1000 Hz! And so it is able to capture micro-expressions, much like the one Mary just made at Frank). Recent scientific research is helping to validate the notion that saccades can be used for communication and annotation (Müller et al. 2009).

One bit of advice for you avatar developers out there: changes in gaze are so fast that is would be wasteful to use interpolation between eyeball rotations. It would just fall between the cracks. Don't bother. And besides, gaze changes, whether for giving the brain snapshots of the world or for throwing flirt vectors, are essentially instantaneous. Biologically-speaking, that's the whole idea. Cartoonists know this well, and willingly teleport not just eyeballs, but whole body parts instantaneously for expressive affect, a notion described amusingly in the Cartoon Laws of Physics (O'Donnell 1980)(Gould 1993).

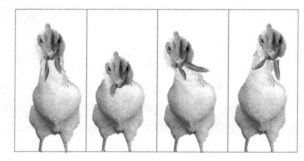

Image: Ventrella

Virtual Gaze

Since real gaze is used for social signaling, and since it serves somewhat predictable communicative purposes, it can be encoded into a succinct representation that allows gaze to be evoked anywhere, anytime, without requiring a physical human head and eyes. I refer to this as *virtual gaze*. Virtual gaze is so powerful that even the *idea* of it, as uttered as commands in text-based virtual worlds, can create visceral responses. Michele White, who studies the ways in which technology renders and regulates users, points out that in text-based virtual worlds, the commands that allow a player to "watch", "scope", "peep", "gawk", etc. can be disturbing to the gazee, especially if she is being continually "looked at" by other players (White 2001).

In animated virtual worlds, gaze is more multidimensional and complex, and has even more potential for powerful effect. For instance, eye rotation could be independent of head rotation. So, an avatar could throw a shifty side-glance with no head motion, or it could gaze with the entire head. The speed at which an avatar rotates the eyes and head to look at something could be adjustable—a parameter roughly associated with "alertness", or "attention". So, if an avatar were tracking a bird fluttering in the air, a "low-alertness" setting would create a rather drunken meandering of the head and eyes in attempt to follow the bird's trajectory, while a high alertness setting would result in quick head/eye motions, keeping a tight aim on the bird the whole time. The same kind of tight alertness response is used in first-person shooters (the camera is very responsive to mouse movement) so that the player can take aim quickly.

A variation of user-controlled gaze was implemented in Second Life in the early days. Richard Nelson (the main avatar designer), and other early developers were exploring interactive techniques whereby the user could "tab" his or her avatar gaze through the set of nearby avatars, analogous to user interfaces that allow the tab key to jump the UI focus through the various elements of an interface, say, for inputting values into fields. This is but one of the many techniques that can be used to set an avatar's gaze, particularly in a social situation in which the gaze targets are clearly defined, and roughly arranged in horizontal order. Other techniques use some degree of automation.

Jumping to a Moving Target and Tracking it

In addition to saccades, there is another kind of eye movement which I haven't mentioned yet. It is called *smooth-tracking* (or *smooth pursuit*). This is what happens when you watch a distant bird arc across the sky. Smooth tracking uses a very different eye-brain control system than saccadic motion.

In virtual worlds and 3D games, one way to establish smooth tracking is to establish a virtual link between the gazer's eyes and the mobile object to be pursued—like the gaze vectors that my make-believe HUD reveals. Remember the chapter on Avatar-Centric Communication in which I showed a picture of circles overlaid onto the heads of avatars? Those were selectable regions where the mouse cursor can be clicked to trigger a gaze shift, causing your avatar to fixate on that avatar's head. Once chosen, this gaze shift would stay fixed even as both avatars moved about in the world. The interaction of passing one's mouse cursor over an avatar's head and then selecting the circle to establish gaze is illustrated below in a simple scene with cats and dogs.

In this illustration, the dog avatar rolls his mouse cursor over the cat at the left. Once the circle over the cat avatar has been selected, the dog avatar will begin to *smooth-track* that cat. (If this were my dog Higgs, he would not settle with just *gazing* at the cat).

The dog avatar selects the cat to establish smooth-tracking (Image: Ventrella)

Recall that in the chapter *A Body Language Alphabet* we explored the notion of sending compact, efficient messages over the internet to evoke complex and meaningful shared experiences. This idea applies very easily to gaze. Imagine yourself sitting on a park bench reading a book. A person walks by and your gaze shifts to the person's face. You continue to track that person for a while, and then your gaze returns to the book. Two salient events have occurred: a gaze-shift to the person, and a gaze-shift back to the book.

Two events: (1) setting your avatar gaze to the passing avatar's face, with tracking, and (2) setting it back to the previous gaze target. (Image: Ventrella)

In a virtual world, these two events could be specified by two messages sent up to the server that specify the identifier of a gaze target (the passerby), followed by a "time-out", or else a specific message to set the gaze back to the book, or some other, new gaze target. Everything that happens in-between those two events does not require any internet messaging, as long as the first message specifies to "track" the gaze target wherever it moves.

All the tracking can be done on the client-side, and that is because the location of the two faces (the *gazer* and the *gazee*) are cached on the local client; they are instantiated in every user's view of the world whose avatar happens to be logged-in at that location, and can potentially see the gazing avatar. All the expensive 3D vector math can be computed locally. If I happen to be controlling the avatar that just walked by, I will see that you have set your gaze on me and tracked me for a while. And the reason I can see this is that your avatar (as instantiated on *my* client) received the gaze message, and my client started running the tracking behavior.

It is not only for technical reasons that a behavior like eye-tracking should happen automatically in an avatar: there really is no need for the user to continually puppeteer this tracking behavior as long as the high-level goal is to "keep looking at the passerby". Now, what about the decision to look at the passerby in the first place? Should that be automated? Like most channels of virtual body language, that would be served best by offering multiple levels of control, each useful at different times and for different purposes. The hardest level of gaze to design, and the easiest to use, is automatic gaze: the avatar system decides when the avatar should shift its gaze, and to whom or what. Ideally, a large set of controls should be tweakable as part of the avatar customization interface, to modulate these automatic behaviors—sort of like "personality filters".

On the opposite extreme, a manual gaze system would be useful for times when the user wants to puppeteer gaze using a short leash: "I want to look at you...*now*".

A virtual world in which users could choose other avatars to gaze at with ease, and to switch that gaze as easily as clicking on the heads of nearby avatars, would become charged with nonverbal energy. The idea of clicking on the heads of avatars is synonymous to directing your attention to various elements on a web site. By clicking on an avatar head, you are saying that you want to look at that avatar (that is, *you* the user, as well as *you* the avatar). If the gazee reciprocates, then you have established a natural, wordless social link. This could be all that's needed (as in two people who simply want to acknowledge each other using eye-contact). Or it could be used as a queue to start a verbal conversation. By allowing this behavior to be operated manually, the social utility of gaze would be entirely up to the users, and they might in fact develop their own nonverbal conventions, forming their own social machinery, without the avatar system imposing a code of behavior. The downside is of course that it requires extra controls, and more attention from the user.

The art of virtual gaze is maturing rapidly. Norm Badler and his co-authors were among the earliest to research the effects of gaze in virtual agents. In many gaze systems, including *SmartBody*, developed at ICT in Los Angeles, gaze is manifested not only in the rotation of an avatar's head, but in the neck, and several joints of the spine. The various ways to look at a gaze target are then adjustable to a fine degree. "Gaze", in this case, need not be a term that applies to the eyes or head only. One can gaze with the whole body, the upper body, the head, the eyes, or any combination, to create many subtle variations of attention or annotation.

Lance and Marcella (2010) have researched the problem of gaze, attempting to map the gaze shifting of a virtual human to particular emotional states, in order to build better models for virtual gaze. Many researchers, like Louis-Philippe Morency, are building systems to detect user head rotation and eye tracking to provide inputs for engaging with embodied conversational agents (ECAs). With the fount of research on embodied conversational agents, social virtual worlds, and remote collaboration, the problem of gaze is now receiving the *gaze* of many thinkers and practitioners.

Avatar body/head/eye gaze in There.com (Image: There.com)

The Shared Social Coordinate System

Human saccades shoot psychic beams with a complex rhythm and symmetry, like visual music playing over the dynamics of verbal communication. Smooth-tracking eyes perform violin sweeps and clarinet glissandos. A virtual world where avatars cannot look at each other is a world without psychic energy; it has no *musical soundtrack*.

Gazeless avatars in *Kataspace* (Image: Katalabs, 2010)

In most virtual worlds it is not easy for users to set the gaze of avatars at will. In Second Life, well-crafted portraits of fashionable residents are often depicted looking off into empty space, which reinforces a kind of persona we often see expressed in these worlds: aloofness and *serene ennui*. Might this kind of persona ultimately be a symptom of a design deficit rather than a conscious artistic decision?

Avatar makers, when they are on computergraphics autopilot, build their avatar rendering code in a similar way as they would other 3D objects in a scene. A consequence of this is that the avatars are not infused with the potential for social or emotional connectivity, and so we end up the current status quo: socially challenged avatars.

When a character animator is composing an animation in a standalone application, the geometry is defined in terms of the character's local coordinate system. For instance, the character's x axis extends from the left to the right of the body. In most systems, the y axis extends vertically: toe-to-head, and the z axis extends from back-to-front. A joint rotation is typically specified in relation to the joint's *parent*. An elbow is rotated *off* the shoulder. An animator may use built-in tools for *inverse-kinematics* (the technique I introduced briefly in

191

Chapter 4) or *forward dynamics* (simulating Newtonian physics for momentum, forces of gravity, friction, etc.) to create special effects—and indeed these procedural animation systems require the temporary use of a coordinate system in a higher frame of reference. But, once the animation is completed, and a file is exported, all joint rotations are normalized to the local coordinate system of the character. It is essentially a record of body movement without a home—without an environmental context—floating in Einsteinian relativistic space.

When this floating animation file is imported into a virtual world and starts running on an avatar in realtime, procedural techniques take charge and help ground the animation in the context of the world. Inverse kinematics in particular is used to modify the leg joints of the animation and adjust them to conform to an uneven terrain as the avatar ambulates through the world. This set of events could never be anticipated during the initial act of animating. Forward dynamics can also be applied to flexible parts of the avatar (hair, tails, etc.) causing them to sag naturally with gravity or shift from wind or collisions with other objects. The same goes with enabling avatar heads to swivel so as to face each other, or for avatars to hold hands…

or…for your avatar to pet-the-virtual-dog…

image: Ventrella

...or to do a hundred other things that ground the motion in the world from moment to moment. Neuroscientists have discovered cells in the brain that they call "place cells" and "grid cells". These cells ground our sense of where we are in the world; they are linked to the hippocampus, and help us incorporate our body schema with the environment (O'Keefe and Dostrovsky 1971)(Hafting et al. 2005). Place cells and grid cells are part of a broad system for dynamic representation of self-location. They can be thought of as the brain's way of coordinating personal space with the global coordinate system. Mirror neurons have their own way of connecting up personal spaces. According to Blakeslee and Blakeslee, they create *shared manifolds of space*: "Watch a fast pass in hockey, listen to a piano duet, or watch two people dance the tango. Mirror neurons help people coordinate joint actions swiftly and accurately, providing a kind of 'we-centric' space for doing things together" (2007).

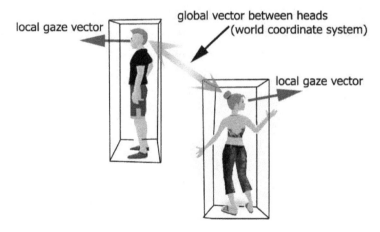

local gaze vector

global vector between heads
(world coordinate system)

local gaze vector

Local gaze vectors must be transformed to the global (social) coordinate system (Image: Ventrella)

The local coordinate system—by itself—is *lonely*. The global coordinate system—the frame of reference which all avatars occupy, and which allows all the various lonely coordinate systems of the world to "transform" to each other—is *social*. The mathematics of social gaze might be described as a *we-centric* connective glue that infuses the social into the personal. Effective virtual body language requires seamless translation between the lonely coordinate system and the social coordinate system. Mathematically-speaking, that means having software interfaces to transform the local geometry of the body to the global geometry of the world.

Gaze Painter – a Game Idea

Here's an idea for a game that could be played in a virtual world (in a virtual field, large stage, or in any area where avatars can move about easily). The basic purpose of the game is to establish *consensual* gaze for as long as possible and with as many avatars as possible over the span of one minute. It involves a handful of players, say about six. Here are the rules of this proposed game: each player's avatar is identified by wearing a colored hat. Each player has the ability to mouse-click on the head of another avatar within view to set his or her gaze to the head of the clicked-on avatar. That player's avatar gaze then stays fixed on the *gazee* even as the two avatars are moving around the space. This is illustrated on the next two pages.

Gaze Painter: the avatar in front establishes mutual gaze with the avatar at left (Image: Ventrella)

Human heads cannot turn completely around (and neither should avatar heads!) So if the gazee is behind the gazer, the gazer will adjust its head as best it can, perhaps even adjusting the spine to compensate. Mouse-clicking on one's own avatar head or some nondescript area in the environment cancels any existing gaze. If a consensual gaze is established (i.e., two avatars are looking at each other) a colored line appears between the avatar heads, corresponding to the color of the player who *initiated* the gaze.

This line remains frozen in 3D space, and designates success by the gaze initiator. If either of the avatars under consensual gaze is moving (i.e., walking, running, flying, falling) then instead of a line, an extruded surface appears—caused by either of the endpoints of the gaze line moving.

New gaze events being added with *Gaze Painter*(Image: Ventrella)

If one of the gaze participants is moving, the line sweeps out a 3D surface (Image: Ventrella)

The more colored geometry a player is able to *gaze-paint* into the 3D space, the higher his/her score. Since extruded surfaces create more color area than lines, players are encouraged to move around a lot or to initiate gaze with avatars who are in motion. You can think of this as a cross between a popularity contest and collaborative sculpture.

Unexpected strategies and behaviors might result. For instance, a kind of *gaze aversion* might arise as a consequence of the rules of the game. I may want to minimize your score by making it harder for you to initiate consensual gaze with me, and so I will avoid looking at you if I think you might already be looking at me. If I "feel your gaze upon me", I will avert my gaze, until the feeling goes away. Then I *pounce*...with my gaze. Variations on the rules of the game might make for some creative strategies for attaining a high score.

Games of this sort might help young people learn some principles of basic geometry as well as acquire sensibilities about social interaction. It might also become a way to create collaborative sculptures or to do virtual performance art.

Four Frames of Reference for my Virtual Body

Now let's go deeper into this concept of local and global coordinate systems. I'd like to propose a general taxonomy of coordinate systems, or *frames of reference*, as a set of possible ways to orient one's embodiment in a virtual world. These are analogous to established points of view in narrative (first person, second person, third person, etc.) Let's go with four. These are illustrated on the next page.

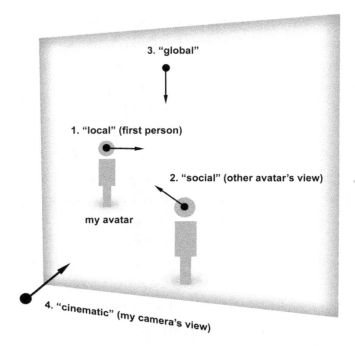

Frames of reference (Image: Ventrella)

These frames of reference are labeled: 1. "local" (my avatar first person view); 2. "social" (another avatar's first-person view); 3. "global" (from the zenith of the environment); and 4. "cinematic" (the camera's view, independent of any other frames of references). Each of these frames of reference has an associated 3D transformation matrix and thus an exact mathematical relationship with the other frames of reference.

From your avatar's local coordinate system, you would see the world from an egocentric point of view—the familiar first-person view; a view that characterizes the me-point of Renaissance Perspective. From the social coordinate system, you would see your own avatar as another user would see you from his or her avatar's local coordinate system (another Renaissance painting, but this one has you in it!) From the global coordinate system, you would see your avatar from a God's-eye-view, as if your avatar were one of many tiny people in a traditional Chinese painting, seen from a stationary vantage point located in some zenith of the virtual universe. No egocentric point of view here.

The last view in this list, the cinematic one, is quite expressive and flexible, and in fact can be seen as a superset of all the others, since it is really a meta-camera that can transform to any one of these coordinate systems and shift between them. For instance, this frame of reference can anchor itself onto your avatar's local coordinate system and then pull backward and upward to become the familiar third-person view. While the virtual camera is often used in this mode— following your avatar around—it may "choose" to perform some cinematic effect, like get out of the way of an obstacle, or zoom-in closer for certain situations. It all depends upon how much cinematic intelligence it has. If the virtual world has a user interface allowing the user to take the camera and move it around manually, this puts cinematic gaze into the hands of the user.

In Virtual Reality (VR—i.e., using head-mounted displays), the camera's gaze is synonymous with the avatar's gaze...which is synonymous with the user's head rotation. When the user rotates his or her head, the view rotates in the same way, with the result being the sensation of full immersion in a scene. This means that in VR, there is no *cinema*. Virtual worlds, on the other hand, are cinematic by necessity. The viewport into a virtual world is typically on a computer screen, which is small within the user's visual field of view (making it less immersive than VR). And users (normally) see their own avatar from a third person point of view: astral-projection—the detachment of cinematic gaze

One way to enhance a social situation is to adjust the camera's distance to the subject as a function of the activity. If that activity happens to be two avatars kissing, it might make sense for the camera to move up close, to indicate the intimacy of the situation. In the prototyping phase of building There.com, we designed the "intimacam", a procedural camera that was aimed perpendicular to the consensual gaze of two avatars, and zoomed-in closer when the avatar heads came closer to each other.

view vector

Intimacam: (Image: Ventrella)

We found the effect of the intimacam to be quite compelling, even though we were working with crude prototype avatars. What the intimacam did was essentially implement the mathematical convergence of three coordinate systems: two avatars and a *voyeur*.

In discussing these various frames of reference, I am exploring the many ways in which one can experience embodiment in a virtual world. When considered as an orchestration of coordinate systems, this brings it in to a mathematical realm, a realm available to software engineering problem-solving. The problems I am referring to are not just philosophical playthings. In fact, some are quite relevant to emerging communication technologies. For instance, take the problem of gaze in video conferencing systems...

Adding Embodiment to Video Conferencing

According to D. J. Roberts of the University of Salford, "Video conferencing faithfully communicates what someone looks like whereas Immersive Collaborative Virtual Environments faithfully represent what they are looking at" (2009). Screenshots of video conferencing participants often show them looking off in random directions—probably at their computer screens—which could be anywhere. And for that matter, their cameras could be anywhere as well. The point is that while each individual may have a clear sense of where the other participants in the conversation are *in their own private desktop views (or laptop views or smartphone views),* this does not translate to a shared visual space.

Video conferencing with multiple participants creates a kind of electronic version of Analytic Cubism, where multiple personal spaces (and gaze vectors) converge onto a single sensory experience. This is illustrated in the collage below of myself Skyping with my colleagues.

Fragmented embodiment and gaze in video conferencing (Image: Ventrella – with permission from participants)

I once noticed while talking with one of my colleagues on Skype that in order to look at the video image of him, I had to NOT look at the camera (located just above the screen on my laptop).

Therefore my eyes were never actually looking straight at him, from his point of view. If I then looked at the camera (so that he might feel as if I were looking at him), I could no longer directly see him to get his reactions to my direct gaze. It's remarkable how people can pick up on the fact that another person is not actually looking into their eyes, but at their chin or off to the side.

Copresence may be strong in video conferencing, but gaze-space remains disembodied and fragmented—just a little too Cubist for comfort. The participants are not only in separate physical locations, they also don't share a *virtual coordinate system*. A number of researchers have explored ways to address the problem of gazelessness in video conferencing (Gemmell et al. 2000)(Yip and Jin 2003), and so we are likely to see some interesting new technologies down the road.

I've been in several work meetings in which some of the participants were remote, joining-in via Skype. I recall one meeting which I attended remotely from home. My colleague called me via Skype and so I showed up on her laptop which was equipped with a microphone, camera, and speakers. My face appeared in a video chat window, and she enlarged it to the full screen so that everyone present at the meeting could easily see me. The group was sitting around a large conference table. As people took turns speaking, my colleague politely rotated her computer around so that I could watch the people as they took turns speaking (and also so that they could see me). My colleague essentially became the equivalent of my avatar *gaze system*, turning my "head" around so that I could participate in the group's weaving of gaze vectors around the table.

Now things are getting really interesting! In this example, the real world and the virtual world were truly melding. A laptop as my "avatar"—how cool is that. This got me thinking that it might be useful to have a conference room specially equipped with extra laptops available, attached to turntables, ready and waiting for any remote attendees to login to a meeting. People present in the room could then provide the polite head-turning actions—keeping the remote people engaged.

Rotating a laptop for assisted gaze in video conferencing (Image: Ventrella)

This is a partial solution at best—but carrying through with this thought experiment might lead to other ideas. For instance, what if I could remotely control the rotation of my turntable? If I could, I would have the freedom to turn my head at will, and face any one at the table (not as quickly as I turn my real head, but on the other hand I would have the supernatural ability to turn my head a full 360 degrees!) I could use wordless body language. For instance, I (that is, *I-the laptop computer avatar*) could turn to face the person next to me, as if to say, "well, what do you think?" I could also turn away from everyone and face the wall to indicate that I am AFK.

Hight-tech video conferencing rooms can make it feel like remote participants are in the same space, gazing at each other. But what about low-tech solutions? These might not be found in expensive hardware and software systems being developed in big companies. The solutions might creep up from behind, outside of the box, as it were, as users spontaneously cobble together their own DIY using the tools at hand. The increased use of mobile computing, smart phones, and iPads might play a role.

Weaving Gaze Vectors Into Our Virtual Spaces

In complex adaptive systems (ecologies, brains, societies, cultures, computer simulations), emergent phenomena arise as a function of component parts (i.e., genes, neurons, people, ideas, software agents) interacting with each other. Key to emergence is *connectivity*: the coupling, and mutual-influence of the parts. If every human were concealed in a box with no input and no output to other humans, there could be no society, no culture. But this is a moot point: humans both generate culture as well as feed on it for survival. Social systems are held together by many kinds of invisible glue. When one form of glue loses its grip and comes undone, people notice.

Without gaze vectors, a shared virtual environment is lifeless: it is missing that potent nonverbal fabric of attention and annotation. If you think about the different modes of virtual body language used for avatars—all requiring varying degrees of technical prowess and engineering time, the simple ability to apply a bit of inverse-kinematics to enable an avatar head to look at another avatar's head is a big bang for buck. I have often wondered why this has not bubbled up to a higher level in the state of the art of virtual worlds and social gaming. Perhaps it is because designing user controls for setting gaze is not so straightforward. The quirky bottleneck of computer keyboards and mice as input devices for actions do not naturally map to gaze behavior. Gaze control may need a more articulated nonverbal alphabet to guide the design of user interaction systems. Indeed, thinkers and practitioners are developing ways to describe, encode, and instantiate this important mode of body language in virtual environments.

Gaze is powerful and efficient, and the effects are highly emergent. And because of the speediness of saccades and the stickiness of smooth tracking, gaze is *dynamic* and *connective*. Once the true dynamic and expressive nature of gaze can be fully woven into virtual worlds, I believe these worlds will come to life like never before.

11

Seven Hundred Puppet Strings

I once had lunch with a very smart computer scientist in the heart of Silicon Valley. He was telling me about an avatar system he was building that incorporated realistic human-body physics. He claimed that it could simulate the physics of relative joint torques and bone masses to an extraordinary level of realism. He believed that it had the potential to become the best avatar system ever made. Throughout his explanation I was giving him congratulatory body language. He was going strong. And then I asked him how he was going to design the avatar's *cerebellum*. He stopped and looked at me as if I had just spoken in alien tongue. Motion control was not something he was prepared to discuss. For him, it was impressive enough to create the software that allowed a virtual human body to obey laws of physics to an exquisite level. The problem of sentience, believability, nonverbal expression, and user control could always be figured out after the (very difficult, and awesomely impressive) physical simulation had been made. Perhaps he had not spent much time thinking about the difference between watching a living, conscious human walk down a flight of stairs, versus tossing a limp marionette down the same flight of stairs.

This chapter is about puppet strings. Not the real ones that marionettes hang from, but the ones that our brains pull to make our bodies move, and the metaphorical ones that cause avatars to move in meaningful ways. Without puppet strings, avatars look dead—even when they have all the physical modeling, gravity, inertia, torques, and frictions that the smart computer scientist was talking about. Dead humans are not very useful or productive as a general rule. Neither are dead virtual humans.

Alas, there *has* been progress in the simulation of sentience in virtual humans. For instance, NaturalMotion is an operation based in Oxford that simulates virtual humans with physical realism, in their software products, *Endorphin*, *Morpheme*, and *Euphoria*.

(Image: NaturalMotion)

I had discussed character control and physics with founders Torsten Riel and Colm Massey on several occasions, back when they were first getting this project off the ground. These guys are masters at *ragdoll physics*; that's a term used to describe the application of physical modeling to virtual humans. Ragdolls are normally innocent and cute, but in this context, the term has acquired a sinister, torture-like connotation. With accurate ragdoll physics, a virtual human falling limply down a flight of stairs can be made to look very realistic. The technique is often used in action games to show horrific deaths. But here's the cool thing: the NaturalMotion engineers have added an important touch to ragdoll physics. They simulate their virtual humans to look as if they are alive throughout their various ragdoll experiences. So, they hold their heads upright, hold their arms out as they fall, and try to keep their balance when tipped over.

In short, their virtual humans have virtual cerebella, vestibular systems, proprioception, and various correcting mechanisms to counter the effects of gravity and inertia. The visual difference is remarkable and very noticeable—owing to the fact that we, the human observers of NaturalMotion's simulated humans, are very good at detecting the subtle cues of living motion.

As I was projecting my congratulatory body language to the computer scientist, I was thinking about the work that many of us (and in particular the folks at NaturalMotion) had been doing for so many years. I had a premonition: he would come up with yet another highly realistic (but *dead*) virtual human. He was perpetuating the uncanny valley. As the technology for building the physics of flesh and bone in humans improves, I become more interested in how to animate these virtual humans. A consensus among many virtual human developers is this: to varying degrees, virtual humans need to *animate themselves*. And the key to self-animation is...*virtual brains*.

The *homunculus*, that weirdly-distorted body map in the brain that I mentioned earlier, appears to be one among many homunculi in the brain, of various shapes, sizes, locations, and degrees of definition. I am reminded of Minsky's *Society of Mind* (the notion of many semi-autonomous agents in the mind whose combination and coordination create the effect of coherent decisions and a sense of self). Your brain is *peopled* with many little bodies! And there is even recent neuroscience indicating that your *peripersonal space* (the arm's-reach sphere of air around you that your gestures occupy) is mapped in your brain as well. The background research supporting these findings is discussed in *The Body has a Mind of its Own* (Blakeslee and Blakeslee 2007).

It seems that the body is *in the brain*, as much as the brain is *in the body*. This might make René Descartes a tad nervous. There are even homuncular maps in the cerebellum, the "little brain", tucked away under the cerebral hemispheres towards the back, important for movement. The cerebellum helps with coordination and in managing the precise timing of actions; it fine-tunes motor activity. It is also involved in motor learning. A theme we will be exploring in this chapter is the notion that learning motor skills over time causes neural structures to get progressively pushed down into lower, less conscious parts of the brain, leaving room for the conscious mind to flow with ease and focus on higher-level decision making. We could use this observation about the brain's motor learning as a guide for designing avatar animation systems, including communication and expression. My argument is this: we not only *could* design avatar animation systems in this way. We *must*. Otherwise, it just won't work.

Homunculi in the cerebellum

The Physical Avatar vs. the Intentional Avatar

Consider human motion the way we experience it in our everyday lives. One day as I was at Turk's Coffee house working on this book, I found myself chatting with a fellow laptop user about the wireless connection in the café. During our conversation, we were looking at each other, making expressions, and pointing to our laptops. Our motions were mostly annotative (pointing to things and setting our gaze). Such gestures are often called "referential practice". They comprise ways in which speakers situate themselves in the world or establish orientation toward objects in the environment or abstract concepts. At one point he looked at the ceiling as he was trying to remember the name of something. Sometimes he would create a visual accent with his otherwise-laptop-pointing hand in the form of a quick waving motion, or he'd flip his hand palm-up for a split second (an abbreviated *shrug*). At no time during this conversation did I consider the fact that his body was held together with bones, ligaments, and muscles. Nor did I want to. He and I were both pure expressive agents. Since he was a living, healthy, coherent human, his motor control system was doing a fine job of obscuring the fact that he is just a physical machine with moving parts filled with pulsating fluids and muscle fibers, allowing him to exist as an agent of pure expression. This is often how we experience one another in our daily lives.

There exists an arrow in humanity that points in a direction away from the visceral and physical, and towards the communicative and intentional, and sometimes the Sublime and Platonic. But if we are helping a friend out of a wheelchair, arm wrestling, or performing surgery, we follow a different arrow that points back in the other direction. Often the Visceral and the Sublime are experienced at the same time. Sex is one example (when it's good).

To realistically simulate human beings, it is important to consider both arrows. For the purpose of discussing avatar motion, let's use the term "physical avatar" to refer to the avatar as an object existing in the virtual world, along with all the other physical objects, and obeying the same laws of physics (to whatever degree the virtual world has physics). And let's use the term "intentional avatar" to refer to the avatar as a communicative agent, whose motions are expressive, meaningful, and goal-directed. In many cases, these motions contradict the laws of physics.

Entropy, and Becoming Virtual

The tendency for a living body to fall with gravity, to age and die, to burn or freeze, is due to its obeying basic laws of physics. Like everything else in the universe, living things tend towards entropy, on average. On the other hand, the tendency of a living body to maintain its structure over time, to craft novel information, to make ordered physical structures, and to generate organized, meaningful sounds and motions, is due to its being alive. The theoretical physicist Erwin Schrödinger said, "The working of an organism requires exact physical laws". He then goes on to say that "living matter evades the decay to equilibrium…it feeds on *negative entropy*" (1944).

Humans have taken the negative entropy principle and are partying on with it like there's no tomorrow. Relatively-speaking, we humans, and the biosphere that created us, are an anomaly. In the vast, mostly silent universe is a tiny—very busy—blue ball called Earth. It expresses a negentropic spike in spacetime (the biosphere), which became much spikier with the evolution of humans. We keep pushing that spike higher and sharper.

Virtual worlds express the human dream to push even farther from the direction of entropy. While virtual worlds manifest many of the physical constraints that we associate with the real world, they also allow metaphysical and supernatural layers of expression (i.e., teleportation, flying, never aging). The most compelling virtual worlds and games strike a good balance between literal physical realism and unbounded creative expression. This is another way of saying that virtual reality is not very useful when it simply aims to replicate physical reality.

Human reality is goal-oriented, emotional, and socially-grounded. Our bodies are meat puppets and our brains are the puppeteers. So, getting back to the subject at hand, I would suggest that simulating the brain (and what the brain does: *mind*) is a good methodology for modeling human reality, with the avatar as the fulcrum.

Pushing Cerebellum Modeling to a Lower Level of Code

In the early years of the SIGGRAPH conferences (Special Interest Group on Graphics and Interactive Techniques), there was much excitement about new rendering algorithms. Invention was happening at a rapid pace. Now, 3D computer graphics rendering is no longer on the cutting edge. Much of it is baked into graphics cards (graphics processing units, or GPUs). When I attended my first SIGGRAPH conference in 1988, physics modeling was a new hot topic. Today it seems that physics is going the way of rendering, and we are now seeing physics cards (PPUs). Perhaps the science of neural processing will eventually make its way into cards as well. Neural Processors will be neatly tucked away, next to the GPUs and PPUs. These "NPUs" might use several key AI schemes, such as neural networks. The baking-in of cognitive modeling might come in stages. Those stages might be roughly associated with the parts of the brain that developed over evolutionary time. Perhaps within several decades we will have baked the functions of the cerebellum into hardware. Embodied virtual agents will be able to perform basic motor actions autonomously— bipedal characters will have a keen sense of balance. After vestibular and body schema modeling, there will be *pain*. Then perhaps an *attention* system, various components of the limbic system, and so on. Eventually there will be enough virtual neural control to imitate the basic motor repertoire of a live human.

But! (and now we come to the main point of this chapter) ...if this neurally-enhanced simulated human represents...*me* (because it's an avatar), how do I control it? I don't want those artificial neurons to be controlling everything. I need at least some puppet strings. What aspects of motion should be within my domain of control? We encountered this question in chapter two. Now we look into it with a bit more detail.

Pulling Cognitive Strings

I have a lovely little duckling marionette. It has four body parts—a head, a body, a left foot, and a right foot. These are made of unpainted wood shapes, and are connected by short, fat nylon ropes. The body parts are simple rounded forms—like the elements in a Miró painting. With only four strings connecting these parts to a simple cross-shaped control, I have mastered this duckling marionette. I can make it waddle along, take clumsy little ducky steps, pause, peck at the ground, and even look up at my friends. But I must say: I am disappointed by the fact that my terrier Higgs is completely unimpressed with my duckling. I thought dogs were supposed to chase birds—or at least take an interest. Perhaps Higgs is not reading the duckling's body language the same way I am, as I project my inner-duckling onto this marionette.

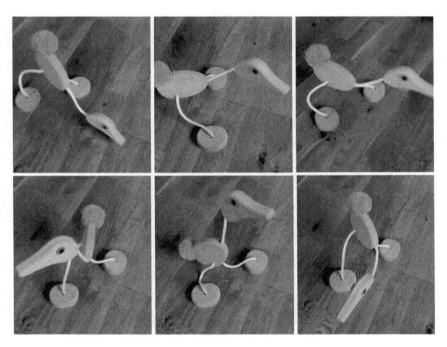

Duckling marionette (Image: Ventrella)

My little duckling is primitive when compared to those beautiful marionettes from Europe, having many more parts, more strings, and more elaborate controls. It takes years of practice to master the art. Skilled puppeteering is not just a matter of having complex puppets with lots of strings and pulling them all at once. It's a matter of knowing how to pull *what* strings—and *when*. Sometimes just a small handful of strings, tugged in just the right way, is all it takes to breathe magic into the puppet. Frank R. Wilson, in *The Hand*, gives a wonderful description of puppetmaster Anton Bachleitner, acting through his marionette, Golem:

"Suspended beneath the trained hands, eyes, and mind of a real master, the movements of a puppet so closely mimic those of a living person that it is a shock to see the puppet alone, off-stage, collapsed, nothing but an inanimate doll. As in real humans, life flows into the puppet's body along barely visible cords that have been called neurons since they were first found in humans. The puppet moves across a tiny stage, alive but ignorant of the true source of its animation, oblivious to its own powerful effects on the thoughts and emotions of those who are watching. A mesmerized neurologist concludes that Bachleitner and Golem are actually communicating with each other and that their bond is intimate. At this moment the technical questions simply evaporate: they *are* each other, so it is no use asking who is really pulling the strings" (Wilson 1998).

Life would be difficult if you had to consciously remind yourself to breathe or to digest your food, or if you had to think about each step you take while walking so you don't fall down. What if every minute action required conscious effort, as if your entire body were a complex puppet, dangling by hundreds of cognitive strings? In a way, your brain (along with the spinal cord) *is* the puppeteer of your body. But not in the same way that I am the puppeteer of my duckling. Consider the fact that the human body has roughly seven hundred muscles. How does the brain manage to puppeteer all those muscles? Of course the brain doesn't *consciously* puppeteer all these muscles, nor does it puppeteer them all at the same time.

Hierarchical Puppetry

Imagine the brain's version of puppeteering as consisting of a vast tree of branching strings. A

society of homunculi and other agents communicate with each other to manage different tasks and perceptions of the body to create the integrated body schema. Some of these various body maps have hierarchical relationships. The premotor cortex has a higher-order body map that manages complex, holistic movements. It is like a higher-order puppeteer.

The notion of using hierarchical modeling for animating human figures has been in the works since the '80s, and was explored in depth by Badler, Barsky, and Zeltzer in the book *Making Them Move* (Badler et al. 1991). Several of the authors featured in the book have designed systems that define multiple levels of abstraction for creating realistic and adaptable animations for virtual humans. Tom Calvert applied concepts of hierarchy and levels of abstraction to the creative process itself, to facilitate tools for animators. Physically-based modeling, inverse-kinematics, and other such techniques have since come a long way, and have consequently been refined and pushed down to the more automatic layers of character animation tools, such as Maya. This means animators can focus on more creative things. It's kind of like how the brain learns skills.

Let's run with this branching metaphor a bit, even though it is an oversimplification of what the brain actually does. The higher cortical layers tug on a few puppet strings at a time; lower levels interpret those tugs and then tug on ensembles of strings the next level down; those tugs cascade down further into more strings. By the time the muscles are stimulated, we're looking at dozens, maybe hundreds, of muscles working in a highly orchestrated way. The most conscious parts are on the top and the least conscious parts are down in the tiny branching twigs of the nervous system (think of the smallest nerve endings). A soccer player running towards a ball might serve as a good example. His attention is focused with Zen-like flow on the ball and getting it to the goal.

The Autonomic Nervous System

The autonomic system is the part of the nervous system that takes care of involuntary actions of your viscera—your stomach, intestines, certain glands, your heartbeat. The autonomic nervous system is vital to survival. Variations of it exist in every animal—and the simplest, most primitive life forms on earth are almost entirely autonomic.

Avatars have autonomic nervous systems. Consider avatar breathing. If you look closely at the avatars in recent 3D virtual worlds and computer games, you can see that there is a constant and subtle heaving of the chest—simulated breathing. This keeps the avatar looking alive. Similarly, without a user doing anything to the avatar, the eyes blink every few seconds, and in some virtual worlds, the head glances around, or its body occasionally shifts. These are the unconscious motions that go on continually throughout the modern avatar's life.

Unlike breathing, walking is a learned behavior. (Ironically, breathing can be *unlearned*: stressed-out, shallow-breathing adults are well advised to try breathing like a sleeping baby). A baby who is learning to take her first step must dedicate great effort and concentration for each step. When a baby is just learning to walk, she has to learn how to pull the low-level puppet strings of her legs. Gradually, she moves up to higher levels—such as, "I want to go over there and stand next to mommy". The lower level string-pulling becomes automatic. Soon enough, walking becomes mostly unconscious, and the baby enters toddlerhood, and the focus shifts towards things in the environment that she can explore. Then comes gymnastics classes. And then if all goes well, the Olympics.

We build these skill layers throughout our lives, constantly pushing what was once conscious and effortful down to the unconscious and effortless, freeing up brain power for higher-level tasks. So, regarding the walking toddler who has grown up and is now an Olympic athlete: is there still a puppeteer in her brain? Yes, but its career has changed. It is more like a manager with several employees handling the details. It now can operate in more intuitive realms. It uses highly efficient neural networks. (If only *all* managers could be described that way).

Back to avatars. When you walk your avatar through a virtual world or computer game, in most cases you are pressing arrows keys or moving a mouse. These are high-level commands compared to controlling the articulated joints of an avatar's legs. Some games and virtual worlds allow the user to click on a certain part of the world which causes the avatar to walk over to that location—an even higher-level action, requiring just a single click. This is how users move their avatars around in IMVU, for example. Every computer game, virtual world, or avatar-based collaboration tool has its own specific purpose, and so, the level of control must be aligned with that purpose. For PacMan, the only user control is turning in one of four orthogonal directions in order to avoid a monster or to eat Pac-dots. The PacMan character is always moving—unless it runs into a wall, so there is no need to control forward motion. Every joystick tug is for the purpose of changing direction. On the opposite extreme, some physics-intensive games require the user to manipulate the body in highly-detailed ways for activities such as scaling a rocky cliff. In this kind of game, missing a ledge could send the character tumbling to a ragdoll death, while finding the right ledges and securing a foot or a hand can get you to the top of the cliff and make a score. In a game or virtual world that requires shifting between high-level navigation and low-level, body-part-specific controls, what is needed is hierarchical puppetry.

Hierarchical Flirting

Let's apply this idea of hierarchical puppetry to the realm of expression and communication. If you wanted to approach the avatar of a friend in a virtual world and let that person know that you are happy to see him or her, you may want to make your avatar smile, or perhaps stand closer. If there is romantic interest, you may use coy gestures, lots of eye contact, or stand in contrapposto, or strike a series of alluring poses. Young teenagers who are new at the flirtation game are sometimes awkward and unaware of their body language. With hormones raging, they unconsciously pick up the cues from each other's body language, which feeds back and generates more unconscious body language. In contrast, experienced adults who play the flirtation game on a regular basis are more aware of their own body language—just as they are more aware of their own verbal language.

In general, how conscious are people of their body language? It varies, of course. Let's look at an extreme case: acting. Actors are professional body language craftspeople. They know how to strike a pose, make a facial gesture, or employ a tone of voice, all in order to articulate a character. But actors are not the only ones skilled in body language: charismatic leaders, politicians, spiritual guides, sex-workers, used car salesmen, and of course, character animators, are skilled at body language. Many professions require skills in nonverbal communication to comfort, encourage, persuade, belittle, amuse, or seduce. And the more skilled at one's own body language a person is, the more puppet strings that person knows how to pull—to become his or her own puppeteer—on multiple layers of the hierarchy. Thus, depending on your profession, your experience, and your intentions, you will puppeteer yourself at different levels of the control hierarchy.

The same principle could apply to avatars. If I want my avatar to be flirtatious with your avatar, I would ideally like to have several options at my disposal—to choose from several layers of the hierarchy. The highest-level option is simply to turn on "flirtation mode", causing my avatar to take on all the appropriate expression automatically. This would be a high-level, mostly hands-off form of flirtation puppeteering, whereby I pull one string (the flirtation string), and all

218

the appropriate strings downstream do the right thing. I should just as easily be able to "release" the flirtation string when my flirt target informs me that her boyfriend—who is wielding a chainsaw—is approaching.

Let's consider the opposite extreme: let's say I just want to wink at your avatar at some point in time when your avatar is looking at my avatar, but only when a rival avatar who is also trying to flirt with you is looking the other way. Furthermore, one half-second after I wink, I want to rotate my right hip to generate a curve in my body profile. In this case, I am watching and waiting…and when the time is right, I act—pulling one low-level string (the left eyelid string), and then another (a right hip rotation string).

These two examples illustrate different levels of puppeteering hierarchy. The first one (pulling the flirtation string) requires the least effort on my part—however, it requires a sophisticated automatic avatar system that generates flirtatious behavior in any given social situation (full-blown AI). The other extreme is more work for me (pulling two low-level strings at just the right time), but it is very easy for the avatar system designer—who merely needs to provide every possible action with a direct controller—no complicated hierarchy or timing mechanisms to design.

The figure on the next page illustrates the idea of moving up and down a puppeteering hierarchy. The example on the left, "wink left eye", entails pulling a single puppet string at the lowest level. The example in the middle entails a more complex gesture—a *shrug*. While it may be easy for the avatar controller to trigger, it involves several puppet strings which must be coordinated to create the right set of motions over some duration of time.

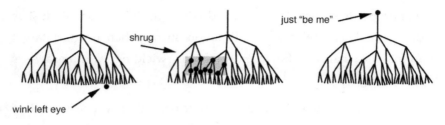

Puppeteering at different levels of the hierarchy (Image: Ventrella)

The Ultimate Avatar Puppet String: "Just Be Me"

The example at the far right shows the highest possible level of avatar control. It is the final puppet string that Pinocchio cut to free himself. If I were a lazy avatar user, or if I were simply too busy to tend to the details, I would yearn to pull the One Puppet String to end all Puppet Strings: the "just be me" string. This puppet string essentially tells an artificial intelligence program to take over and act as a stand-in for me. It knows when to pull the flirtation string and it knows when to pull the annoyed string; it knows when to run away and when to attack; it knows how to do everything—exactly as I would do it if I were controlling the avatar. It even knows how to chat, and use the same verbal language that I use. This AI is of course difficult, maybe even impossible, to design—at least for the next several decades.

Pneumatic Puppetry

Have you ever seen one of those inflatable blow-up dancing figures out in a parking lot or on top of a building? They are sometimes called "Inflatable Wavers", and they are good at attracting attention. That's the whole idea: they are used to pull in the public eye for advertisement.

An inflatable waver (Image: Ventrella)

These animated figures employ one puppet string in the form of forced air blowing upward and filling the column-shaped balloon. Thanks to nonlinear dynamics and the properties of the material used, these balloon dancers flop upward with endlessly novel surges of glee. This illustration above shows several snapshots that I took of one of these figures not too far from my home. The floppiness is engineered to look like a dancing skinny figure waving its arms and announcing to the world that something great is happening nearby. The arms occasionally bend and create momentary gestures—which are meaningless. But as I watch it perform, I can easily imagine myself performing these gestures. It is not hard to imagine a child watching one of these things and dancing along with it.

Great comedians, actors, dancers, and animators employ secondary motion—manifestations of floppiness, jiggles and wiggles—to create extra layers of motion that can either serve to evoke sheer excitement and raw energy, or to add short-lived, nuanced meaning to their body language. It's a touch of ragdoll physics. This upward-blowing inflatable waver could be considered as a ragdoll of sorts. Now let's look at an application of ragdoll physics that is a just a bit :) more complex than the inflatable waver.

Physical Avatar Puppeteering

When I first started working at Linden Lab, CEO Philip Rosedale and I would discuss ways to make the avatar seem more natural. He would say, "Wouldn't it be cool if I could just walk up to your avatar and give it a little push, and it would respond naturally?" Then he would give my shoulder a little shove, just to point out what would happen: the rest of me would lurch, and I would have to catch myself to not tip over (CEOs are allowed to do this). This level of avatar-to-avatar interaction is exactly what I had wanted to work on. This was my motivation to develop *Physical Avatar* Puppeteering.

But there was another—more communication-focused—motivation. It goes like this: while chatting with your avatar friends, do you ever wish you could just click the mouse cursor on your avatar's head, wobble the mouse, and make your avatar nod yes? Or no? Perhaps you might want to tilt your avatar head for some affect, like, "I'm giving some thought to what you are saying", or, "Huh?", or "Aren't I cute?" Maybe you might want to do the Indian head waggle, or hold your chin up with pride. And wouldn't it be great if you could alternate between these actions as easily and nearly-unconsciously as you normally click around on a web page, move windows, and drag files around on a desktop interface? Why can't the avatar's body have as many direct controls as a standard desktop interface?

The motivation and overall goal was clear, but the path to execution proved to be quite difficult. This is partly because the standard avatar skeleton is *hierarchical*, and so are all the animations. Hierarchy—the structural property of systems in which some parts are *above, more important, more general*, or *more in control* than other parts—is useful for some applications, but too constraining for others. Earlier I referred to hierarchy in the brain—admittedly an oversimplification, but a workable model for managing complexity in a virtual human). In the case of applying procedural animation to an avatar skeleton, hierarchy imposes constraints that have to be circumnavigated. This was the case in developing the avatar puppeteering system. (As of the writing of this book, the source code for Avatar Puppeteering is available in the Second Life viewer source repository, and it is described in the Second Life Wiki page (Linden Lab, 2009)).

To achieve the goal of more fluid, environmentally-connected responsiveness in the avatar, I had to build a physics layer on top of the existing avatar code. This layer enabled a user to tug at individual joints of an avatar—essentially to puppeteer the avatar with fine detail, using a direct manipulation user interface. I wanted to wire-up the avatar with metaphorical puppet strings, and give it a physical representation (like ragdoll physics but without the gravity part).

Using Physics for Expression

By replacing the avatar's hierarchically-arranged joints with balls connected by spring forces, the whole body would stay together, due to the simultaneous forces of all the springs continually acting on all the balls. So, when tugging on a ball (like the elbow shown here), the neighbor balls would get pulled along. Everything was connected with equal priority. This *removal of hierarchy* was considered a necessary step in order to *re-introduce* hierarchy—only this time with more expressive potential. Let me explain this in more detail.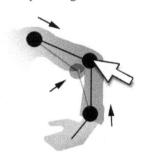

The illustration on the next page at left shows a thigh bone represented as a spring force (white line), holding the knee and hip balls together (at thigh-length distance). The image in the middle shows all the springs, and the image at right shows some extra internal springs added in the chest and pelvis areas for reinforcement.

You may be familiar with Hooke's Law, the equation whose constant k determines the force of a spring. This constant, with the addition of other constants (i.e., for friction), can be adjusted to create a very stable spring force that acts more like a semi-rigid bone than a jelly worm. *Physical Avatar* has carefully-tweaked spring constants to define a stable skeleton rig upon which the Avatar Puppeteering feature was developed.

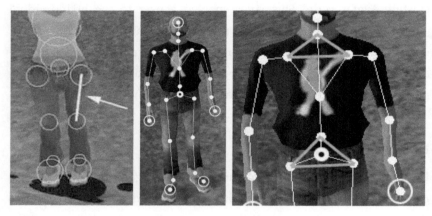

Using a spring-based skeleton rig for a direct-manipulation interface (Image: Ventrella)

The interaction scenario worked like this: if the user held down the CONTROL key and then moved the mouse cursor over his/her avatar, translucent dots would appear over the joints as the mouse cursor passed over them. This provided affordance and discoverability: "hmm—I see a dot. I think I'll click on it to find out what happens". If the user then clicked on a dot, my software would wake up and immediately construct a balls-and-springs rig that replicated the exact world-coordinate system positions associated with the hierarchical skeleton.

Then, as the user dragged the mouse cursor around, still holding the mouse button and CONTROL key down, the avatar joint (a ball in 3D space) would get moved around, and because it was connected by springs to neighboring joints, they would get moved as well, kind of like what happened when Philip gave me the shoulder shove.

The image below shows an avatar being posed. There are orientation indicators shown (used for testing purposes).

An avatar posed using Physical Avatar (Image: Ventrella)

A Few Technical Details

In standard hierarchical animation, a rotation in the ankle joint causes the foot to pivot and this causes the toes to move to a new position. There is essentially no need to specify a *toe joint position* because all the foot geometry can be determined completely from knowing the ankle rotation and position. As a consequence of not having a toe joint, it is not possible to *grab* the toe and move it in order to rotate the ankle (that requires something like inverse kinematics). *Physical Avatar* is basically a variant of inverse-kinematics, achieved through physical simulation. In order to grab a toe, or the tip of the hand,

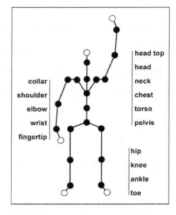

or the top of the head, extra joints were needed (five, to be exact). These are called "end effectors" and they add five extra joints to the default 19, bringing the total number of avatar joints to 24

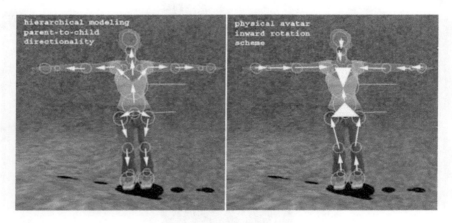

Hierarchical animation trickles-out of the local coordinate system: *Physical Avatar* trickles-in the global coordinate system (Image: Ventrella)

In order for *Physical Avatar* to be fused with the existing hierarchical animation system so that it could be turned on and off at any time, it needed to perform a series of mathematical somersaults. It had to convert the hierarchical representation into the physical representation (so that the various physical effects and user-manipulations could be applied). It then had to be re-mapped back to the hierarchical representation (the hard part!) so it could be rendered in the usual way. This all had to happen in real time.

Physical Avatar enables general ragdoll physics effects. It's not that we needed to see the avatar get flopped around realistically like monsters being slaughtered in a first-person shooter. The ragdoll physics layer basically gives the avatar a larger vocabulary of motion, including motions for expressivity and creativity. A shove of the shoulder, a slap in the face, a hug, a slump from being tired, a strong gust of wind, doing the hippy dance; all these effects could be overlaid on top of the standard animation layer with the help of the ragdoll layer. These effects make the avatar resonate with the physical simulation within which it is embedded.

(Image: Ventrella)

And okay, I admit, an avatar-catapult-throwing game with full-on ragdoll physics would be pretty awesome.

From One Puppet String: Many

You may be wondering how this technique compares with the ragdoll state-of-affairs I described earlier with the smart computer scientist. Well, in fact, my physics algorithm was far less realistic than his, and so it certainly didn't have that going for it. The difference is in intention. Every line of code that I wrote was written with a mantra for making the avatar more *expressive*. And so, various constraints were added to allow a user to move joints around and to keep things in a reasonable configuration so as to make interaction intuitive and natural.

Regarding this idea of clicking on the head to nod yes or no, a puppeteering act need not be a "tug" in a certain direction, as if there were a string attached or as if a joint were being grabbed and moved. Puppeteering a body part can also be a *rotation* (like turning a knob). Rotation is always performed around some axis. In the case of the head, that axis determines whether you are nodding yes, nodding no, or doing the waggle. It gets complicated rather quickly when trying to figure out what kinds of controls to give the user for easy expressive rotations (a good place to see well-crafted examples of this is in high-end character animation packages).

With the collaborative contributors Aura Linden, Qube Linden, and others helping out on the project, we invented other uses for this algorithm. Aura had devised a scheme by which a user could create a series of full-body poses, save each one in memory, and then use these as keyframes for generating whole animation sequences. The benefit of this way of making avatar animations was that the user wouldn't have to leave the virtual world, open up a separate animation software package, build an animation using some alien avatar, and then import that alien's animation back into the virtual world. Aura's scheme allowed a user to construct an animation entirely in-world, in the context of all the surrounding ingredients that would give that animation meaning.

We had also worked on ways to create symmetric puppeteering, whereby moving a joint would cause the joint on the opposite side of the body to move in the same way. Take this idea to another level: imagine clicking and dragging the mouse to generate more complex actions that involve several joints, coordinated to generate many whole-body expressive stances. In short, you don't have to think of puppeteering as an act of pulling a single string at a time.

So, as you can see, even though *Physical Avatar* used a low-level form of physical simulation, the ultimate goal was to allow bootstrapping to higher, more expressive controls. But this feature never got past the stage of the proverbial baby learning to take its first step. These things take time.

I haven't even mentioned the networking considerations—how to make a puppeteered avatar animate accurately on remote viewers over the internet. After all, what good is expressing with your avatar if your movements can't be seen by others? This was out of my line of expertise, and certainly not a piece of cake for the engineers on the project who knew a thing or two about server communications, and labored for months to get that aspect working. This is one of the reasons the project was stalled.

But there's a more fundamental reason: Linden Lab was not the right place to realize an avatar puppeteering system of the scale that I was attempting. At that time, the company was thrashing over serious technical issues like server crashes—a very consuming problem. And because of the management structure, Linden Lab was not well-suited for simultaneously supporting critical engineering efforts along with more long-term development efforts.

There is another reason: at the time, the most talented engineers were occupied with developing a new rendering system that allowed for more realistic lighting effects. In the end, attraction to bright lights and implementing algorithms that make things sparkle won-out over developing tools to enhance avatar expressivity.

I've gone on quite a bit about "pulling puppet strings", but if I'm referring to using computer keyboards and mice, what exactly constitutes the *strings*? Puppeteering of course is not just about pulling strings, nor is it necessarily about jabbing keys or pushing mice (or rubbing iPad screens). In previous chapters, we looked at some techniques for triggering expressions and gestures in avatars within the realm of typewriter ergonomics. But these interfaces are awkward at best, especially when considering that nonverbal movements are often associated with speaking—they are *coverbal*. Even more challenging:

the creation of nonverbal movement would have to be generated simultaneously with the creation of words, if it is to come across as natural. And if you're busy typing on a keyboard, then your hands are too busy to puppeteer. Well, there's one solution to the problem of generating both words and gestures at the same time in a natural way, and that is to use the *voice* as the puppeteer. That is what the next chapter explores.

12

Voice as Puppeteer

In chapter three I mentioned Gestural Theory—which states that speech emerged from the communicative energy of the body: from iconic, visible gestures. It has been found that the regions of the brain responsible for mouth and hand movements are sitting right next to each other. It is well established that sign language is just as sophisticated as any spoken language in terms of grammar. And sign language communicators appear to use the same language areas of the brain. A possible scenario that supports Gestural Theory goes something like this: as our ancestors made the evolutionary transition to walking on two legs, their hands were freed up for gestural communication. Chimpanzees provide a good illustration for this transition; they frequently switch between four-legged and two-legged locomotion (quadrupedalism and bipedalism). Bipedalism frees up their "front legs" for gestural expression. As our ancestors evolved further, those expressive "front legs" were used increasingly for tool manipulation—and this created evolutionary pressure for vocal sounds to take over as the primary language delivery method. The result is that we humans can walk, use tools, and talk, all at the same time.

The contemporary human mind swims in a sea of abstract symbols, propelled by the advent of written language…which is based on speech…which arose from gesture (according to Gestural Theory). A transitioning from analog to digital continues today with the spread of the internet over the biosphere. But even as the evolutionary vector of communication points away from physical and embodied and towards digital and symbolic, it doesn't follow that we are trying to escape our physical origins. Digital-alphabetic-technological humanity has an opportunity to reach down to its gestural underbelly and invoke the rich primal energy of communication. There's a good reason to reconstitute natural language virtually, because we are sitting on top of a heap of alphabetic evolution that has been forming for thousands of years. The very technology that has created so much isolation between us might be used to bring us back to physical bonding—virtually at least.

Here's an idea: craft an inverse of the gesture-to-speech vector that Gestural Theory posits. Articulate the vector and its environment, and then build a bridge back to gesture. It is a way to put our bodies back into our communications as we spend more time on the internet, spewing and consuming disembodied verbal language. It's about reconstituting gesture virtually, using *speech*.

The Argument for Voice-Triggered Body Language

Gesticulation is the physical-visual counterpart to vocal energy. We gesticulate when we speak—moving our hands, head, and other body parts…and it's mostly unconscious. Humans are both verbally-oriented and visually-oriented. Our brains expect to process visible body movement when we hear spoken words, even if the speaker is not visible. In fact, neurologist Terrence Deacon suggests that the brain's auditory processing of speech is based on the gestural production of sounds and the original vocal energy, rather than the acoustical attributes of the sounds (Deacon 1997). It is almost as if our brains had evolved to understand visible gesture, and then had re-adapted for auditory gesture, on the path to processing spoken words.

Let's consider gesticulation and its intimate relationship with audible speech as the basis for an avatar animation algorithm called "voice-triggered gesticulation". We will use this as a springboard to come up with more advanced techniques for reconstituting the whole spectrum of human nonverbal movement, as a function of the spoken word. But first I want to spend some time talking about lips.

Lip Pixels

When I was an avatar developer, I had a recurring déjà vu experience. It goes kind of like this: I'm having a conversation with a colleague at work. It could be an engineer, could be a designer—doesn't really matter. I'm telling this person about my work on avatar expression, and I announce that I'm working on voice-triggered animation. Immediately my colleague says, "Cool! So, you're doing lip-sync!"

Uh, no. That's not what I'm doing.

Let's talk about pixels. In a typical view of an avatar in a virtual world, the number of pixels that avatar occupies on the screen is considerably smaller than the number of pixels that are in the surrounding scene. Let's imagine that I have walked my avatar up to another avatar, and I have initiated a conversation with that avatar. For the sake of illustration, based on the distance of my avatar's camera to the other avatar, it occupies, say, 20% of the total pixel real-estate of the computer screen. That avatar's head occupies less—let's put it at 5% of total pixel real estate. And the avatar's mouth occupies even less. Let's go with 1%.

Of course I'm making up these numbers, but we can be pretty confident that the number of pixels that an avatar's mouth occupies is quite small. So, it would follow that if those pixels changed as a result of lip-sync animation, the visual effect would be negligible, as compared to movement in the avatar's whole body.

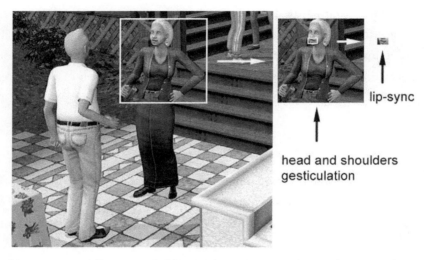

Lips occupy a small percentage of the visual space in a typical view of a simulated character (screenshot from *The Sims*: © Electronic Arts)

Now let's consider what Pixar animators typically do when they're developing a character for an animated feature film. In the beginning, the character's overall body movements are fleshed-out—the movements of that character in relation to other characters, the broad gestures, etc. The overall choreography is crafted to help carry the narrative. Then, the animators come back and refine the characters more by working on facial expressions. Then, as a final pass, they work on the mouth. (An exception to this rule might be when there is a close-up shot of a character's face). Character animators are masters at visual storytelling; they know how to take command of the entire visual canvas to push the storyline or articulate a character's development. Whole-body language is key. And unless we're talking Jabba the Hut, mouth animation is going to play a relatively minor role.

So, why this assumption that I am doing lip-sync when I tell people that I am working on voice-triggered animation? I have a hypothesis: why did good old-fashioned AI not live up to the promise of making machines think, or at least reliably simulate human intelligence? It is because of a major distraction. People are obsessed with words (especially highly educated people who read, write, hear, and speak huge quantities of words...including AI software programmers). Since the sounds of words emanate from the mouth, the obvious body part to focus on is the mouth—*that thing that moves when you talk.* "Visemes" are the facial and oral positions and movements that are simultaneous with "phonemes": the smallest audible components of speech that can convey meaning. Of course the reading of visemes for understanding speech is sensible and practical, especially for deaf people who rely on lipreading to a significant degree. But in distinguishing verbal language from nonverbal language, how would you classify mouth shape and movement used for understanding speech? I am more likely to place lipreading into the verbal language bucket. And since my primary goal in developing a voice-triggered gesticulation system was to generate nonverbal language, I was not so concerned about lips.

Rubber Mask

I am both amused and weary of visually realistic, "cutting edge" facial animation technologies. Sometimes every pore on the skin and every hair follicle can be seen. In some cases the only thing that is animated is the mouth (sometimes the eyebrows). For some reason, teeth are often rendered in a ghastly stark white—and so if there are any slight blemishes in the lip geometry when the mouth is closed, specks of icy-cold white peek out from behind.

Worse: the head is sometimes motionless while the lips move, as if it were locked in a vise. Scientific investigators are in the habit (a good habit in most cases) of eliminating as many extraneous variables as possible in controlled experiments, so as to clearly analyze the behavior, feature, or phenomenon in question. But what if the subject being studied is inherently multimodal...like human expression? Emotion? Perception? Eliminating degrees of freedom, aspects of the surroundings, or the context for human behavior and response doesn't always help matters. Sometimes all it does is make people uneasy. A creepy head-in-a-vise can ruin the whole party—scientifically speaking.

I recall sitting in design meetings with my avatar developer co-workers. Half-daydreaming, I would watch my colleagues' head motions, hand gestures, postures, and the 3D rhythm of their saccadic vectors. Sometimes I would become so fixated on these movements—in a trance—that I would forget what we were talking about. This habit did not serve me well in grade school, nor did it serve me well in company meetings. But it made me especially sensitive to the nuances of body, head, and face motion as a function of speech. Whenever I saw a new face animation demo that put the virtual human's head in a vise and showed only lips moving (badly), I would get the uncanny willies. My viscera would protest. I would react so strongly that I would appear a tad out of control—causing a disruption to the team's studious exploration of avatar research.

Lip-sync in animated films with non-human characters (rendered realistically) can also look out of sorts—in a *rubber mask* sort of way. The rubber mask effect is the result of facial animation systems that don't differentiate between the degrees and directions of movement on various parts of the face. When an *expression morph* causes all the geometrical vertices near the morph control points to shift as if they were all made of the same flexible material—total rubber mask effect results. This is one rationale for using flat-shading (or high ambient shading with low-contrast textures) on the face. Strong textures tend to reveal the imperfections of facial animation, while flat-shading or soft textures recede more to the background, and allow the sharper features (with higher expressive currency) to pop out—like eyebrows, eyelashes, the edges of the face, the hairline, and the lips.

There will come a time when both facial animation and realtime phoneme detection are at the level where lip-sync becomes convincing (or otherwise non-creepy). The facial movement of the Na'vi people in *Avatar* may have set the bar for what computer-generated facial animation will need to be before the uncanny valley can be crossed. However, as I pointed out earlier, real human actors generated the Na'vi mouth motions, along with audible speech and whole-body language, so this does not serve as an example of lip-sync. Compare this expensive blockbuster film to an online virtual world in which the voice of an average, non-actor user has to be mapped to some representation, like phonemes, which in turn has to drive the facial animation of an avatar in realtime (more than 20 frames per second). In a film like *Avatar*, a single frame of animation can take hours to generate. The number of polygons employed in animating a sneer or a trembling lip could be large indeed. It would be unrealistic to ask a user to put on a high-end motion capture set up. And even if this were done, there is the problem of lag: if the facial animation lags behind the user's speech by a fraction of a second, the effect would be disconcerting.

Douglas Gayeton, creator of the machinima film, "Molotov Alva and His Search for the Creator", chose not to tackle the lip-sync problem, due to the poor avatar animation available in Second Life. Gayeton employed a lot of "thinking" avatar scenes: the thoughts are implied by voice-over monolog. There are even several scenes in which the characters in the film are either speaking to the viewer or to each other. In all cases, no lip-sync is used. Even if it had been made available to Gayeton with some reasonable level of functionality, it would likely have degraded the cinematic quality.

Consider that character animators often start with the broad, narrative-enforcing body gestures as a first pass, come back to facial expressions as a second pass, and finally animate the lips. My choice to leave out the last step was based on the degree of expression it affords versus the amount of work required to make it look reasonable. Would I recommend leaving out this last step now—a decade after that rash of déjà vu experiences? Probably not. Avatar animation is more advanced now. Also, if you see a character move its body naturally in response to a voice, yet there is no mouth animation, you may get an uncanny effect. My attempts at avoiding the uncanny valley by focusing on body movement alone could backfire. But perhaps I should not belabor this point any further. Rather than worry about whether to animate mouths or whole bodies, let's just step back and consider the question of control; that's the wicked problem that we keep hitting up against. Whatever part of the avatar we want to animate, we need to attach puppet strings and devise a way for users to pull them intuitively. Here's the key: the voice not only provides an easy and natural signal for realtime puppeteering; it also has infinite potential regarding semantic interpretation.

Voice Chat and Gesticulation

In the beginning of the book I introduced the early virtual world, *Traveler*, which permitted users to speak into microphones and chat naturally. Steve DiPaola invented some techniques for Traveler which caused the voice to animate the floating faces that served as avatars. Since the developers of Traveler were using fairly abstract avatars by today's standards, in a way they had more artistic freedom. And so they used a lip synch animation technique that took voice signals and mapped them to phonemes (Dipaola, 2008). Since they were dealing with floating heads, they didn't have much choice! But Steve did better than that; he used certain attributes of the voice to animate the eyebrows as well. He acknowledged that the "thing that moves when you talk" is not just the mouth, it's the whole face. Steve had created one of the earliest examples of voice-triggered gesticulation in avatars.

Years later, when voice chat was introduced into There.com, I invented a similar technique for voice-triggered gesticulation. By that time, our avatars had become slightly more realistic than those of prior virtual worlds, such as Active Worlds and Traveler. Imagine hearing real people's voices emanating from realistic avatars, but with no associated movement. When I first witnessed this in a demo, I got the uncanny willies in a big way. Being the body language geek that I am, I got up on my gesticulation soapbox and started a campaign to add voice-triggered animation. And yes, I did a lot of hand-waving in the process.

My strategy was to use atomic units of gesticulation and to allow the jumps in sound amplitude from the voice signal to trigger these various atomic units, similar to what was used in Traveler. Tracking the amplitude of the voice signal at about 10Hz, I would identify when there was an upward trend in amplitude within that time duration, and use this as a triggering event. Small jumps in amplitude would trigger subtle movements in the head. Medium jumps in amplitude would cause larger head movements and some hand movements. And big jumps in amplitude would cause the whole upper body to shift or lurch, sometimes involving both arms to pop up with Sicilian staccato. The tweaking of these thresholds was anything but scientific! Because of the mess of factors involved (human factors complicated by unpredictability in microphone performance etc.), these thresholds were smushed around until it worked best in most situations ("smushing", I might add, is an *Art*, refined to the highest degree by the likes of Claude Monet, Walt Disney, and Tom Waits ;)

When triggered, these gesticulation units were slightly randomized, to avoid repetition and robotic regularity. They were allowed to overlap for smooth transitioning (one gesticulation might start while another is still in motion). Animation blending helped keep the phrasing smooth and continuous if the units occurred in rapid succession. Now, you may be wondering: how can such a simple, braindead animation scheme work? There is no intelligence to these gesticulations! Well, you just have to see it in action. At the most basic level, a human body that moves more when it is talking more loudly is much more realistic than one that doesn't move at all. Just this in itself goes a long way in terms of making an avatar look like a user is talking through it.

Speech to Text to Body Language

In this book, I have described several ways that users can or could puppeteer their avatars. The collision of text chat with 3D animation that I mentioned earlier has necessitated many innovations—none of which can ever really circumnavigate the incongruence of creating text on a computer keyboard and having that trigger animated expressions. These two modalities occupy different spacetime dimensions. Gesticulation is not associated with the generation of text; it is associated with vocalization. Gesticulation and vocalization evolved together.

If I had to hire a puppeteer for my avatar's body language, I would choose a living voice rather than hands fumbling over a keyboard.

There's another reason to consider voice as puppeteer: with speech-to-text software becoming more sophisticated, and natural language processing continuing to advance, it is more feasible to extrapolate rich meanings from words, phrases, and sentences. Add to that the many cues from prosody: voice intonation, pauses, etc. These can become triggers for any number of gestural emblems, postures, stances, facial expressions, and modulated gesticulations. And, yes, lip sync.

If the user is tired of talking, doesn't want to wake up the sleeping children, has a speech impediment, or is completely unable to speak, then keyboard text entry could be inserted, bypassing the speech-to-text part of the pipeline. A good bit of puppeteering punctuation might be needed in this case, to compensate for the absence of prosody. This approach could even involve converting the user's text to synthetic speech if the members of the chat group prefer to keep their verbal language in the audible realm.

Motion-Capture for Teaching an Avatar Your Nonverbal Personality

Voice filters are available in some voice chat systems to mask a user's identity for role-playing. For instance, a man can sound like a woman, or vice versa. The timbre of your voice can be altered, allowing you to engage in *theatre*, play... identity-transformation. Imagine a system that also filters your body language and reconstitutes it in an avatar that mimics the unique motions of a specific communicative act. What if avatars had mirror neurons?

Here's a possible future scenario to consider: You put on some motion capture markers. As we saw with the Gestural Turing Test, it doesn't take more than a handful of markers in key locations on your body to pick up the salient motions for most communicative body language. Alternatively, camera vision systems may become so advanced that motion capture markers will become a thing of the past (witness Microsoft's *Kinect* for the Xbox 360). In either case, suppose that your head and hand motions can be picked up in real-time. Now, you select an option on the avatar control panel called "watch me and learn". Then, you engage in natural conversations with other people, making sure to let it all hang out, letting your head and hands move freely, etc. While you speak, the sounds you generate are parsed into text. The motions you make are stored in a database with the associated text. As these motions and associated texts are collected, your avatar starts building a vocabulary of identifiable gestures, postures, and so-on. It starts associating those patterns with specific words and phrases that you spoke while generating the body language.

Can a *nonverbal idiolect* be captured in a database? (Image: Ventrella)

This idea is not new. Researchers have developed several techniques and experiments whereby gestural data is collected from performers, or even from analyzing video segments, and then later reconstituted in virtual humans to accompany the production of verbal language. This research shows promise for becoming the basis for effective auto-gesticulation systems.

The illustration on the next page shows a few hand gestures researched by Michael Neff and colleagues (2008), indicating how the unique gestures of an individual can be captured and then reconstructed in a form that can be played back with modifications to accompany the original spoken word, or associated text.

Hand gestures accompanying speech – top: "cup"; bottom: "progressive" (Image: Neff)

The top image shows a straight vs. curved trajectory of a "cup gesture" (palm up with mostly horizontal motion). The bottom image shows a "progressive" (the speaker's hand revolves, referring to the abstract notion of a forward rotating wheel which in turn refers to a word like "going", or "developing"). This progressive shows some translation upward and rightward, as indicated by the looping arrow. The timing of gestures like these, in addition to when they happen in association with words, their directions of motion, and whether they occur at all—are all ingredients in one's nonverbal idiolect.

Regarding the buildup of gestures: it doesn't have to stop at the nuances of speech itself. The system could take into account environmental situations (to whom you are talking, where you are in the world, what events have recently happened, etc.) As the database resolves into focus, a "nonverbal idiolect" emerges in your avatar's memory banks. (While "dialect" refers to the unique language variety of a people, "idiolect" refers to the language style of a single individual. I use "nonverbal idiolect" to refer to an individual's unique body language).

Continuing on with this scenario: imagine that you return to the virtual world, and—without requiring any motion detection—you see that your avatar has begun to take on some of your unique body movements. At any time, you would be able to switch on the motion detection apparatus, and train your avatar more. This would be an iterative scheme: there would be no final state of correct behavior; no ultimate conversational style that your avatar would converge upon. You would always be able to re-train your avatar with new kinds of body language, thereby causing it to unlearn previous body language behaviors, or at least have those subsumed by more recent body language. You could have an interface that allows your avatar to "wear" different versions of your own nonverbal idiolect. For instance, if you are talking to your boss, you probably don't want to wear the same nonverbal idiolect that you would wear if you are on a hot date (unless your boss is the hot date).

There could be another option that allows your avatar to pick up the nonverbal idiolect of the avatar you are talking to (whose nonverbal idiolect may have been learned by another avatar, and so-on: a *hall-of-mirror-neurons*). Perhaps there could be a "chameleon" slider on the interface that determines how easily and quickly your avatar takes on new nonverbal idiolects. There may be intellectual property concerns with having one's personal movement signature used (or "stolen") by someone else. This kind of blurring between *property* and *personhood* is expounded upon by some pundits (de Andrade, 2009).

Once recorded, the nonverbal idiolects of many kinds of people could be uploaded into a library. This is an idea that Judith Donath of MIT has expounded upon. Just as easily as buying avatar clothes or body types, you could buy the behavioral personalities of Persians, Chileans, Chinese schoolboys, 90-year old Ethiopian women, Alfred Hitchcock, or Bugs Bunny. Or your spouse. Or yourself from last year when you were on medication. Or yourself yesterday when you were in an especially confident mood.

Go to your voicemail. Listen to a message that a close friend left for you. As you listen, you can easily imagine that person's facial expressions while leaving the message. You might also imagine that person's head and hand motions. You can imagine this because you have that person's nonverbal idiolect cached in your brain. That's what I want to see actualized in a voice puppeteering system.

13

Looking Ahead

In this final chapter I will try to make a soft landing (though I'm a relatively new pilot so please buckle your seatbelts). I want to look at current technologies for conducting nonverbal communication, and consider some future technologies. And then I'll make some concluding remarks.

There are many ways for people to combine verbal and nonverbal language and conduct these communications over the internet. And the number of ways is likely to increase. Following is a list of communication modes, some of which we have touched upon in this book. Some of these are very much here and now, and others are still incubating in minds and research labs. Each includes some form of distributed body language.

1. Telephony

I'm referring to traditional phones and mobile phones, as well as voice over internet, and all variations therein. Talking on the phone includes nonverbal communication: not only are words generated, but also the prosody—the intonations, pauses, ums and uhs—the musical dynamics of speech which accompany the pneumatic force to expel words. This is body language in the form of sonic gesture.

2. Video Chat Plus Telephony

Now add a camera to the phone. This is your basic Skype, or any one of the several video chat applications. It's Voice plus Video. It is powerful, useful, and here to stay, because it brings visible body language into the mix. As we have explored in the book, it does not afford the plasticity of avatars in virtual worlds, and the expressive possibilities. It is a broadcast medium that replicates one's appearance and sounds at a distance.

By the way, have you ever had the experience of being in a Skype conversation with someone, and her camera doesn't work but yours does? She can see you but you cannot see her. It's awkward, isn't it? You'd rather just stick with voice and no visuals, right? That's because your friend has an advantage over you; she can read your body language, but you cannot read hers. She may use a modality of conversation that relies on visual signals, and thus not put as much effort into the verbal aspect, leaving you in the dark, as it were.

3. Text Chat

I am referring to writing and receiving text at near-conversation rates; this includes instant messaging and mobile texting. I mention this modality because, unlike traditional reading and writing, text chat is conversational and spontaneous. The rhythm of the back-and-forth of texting constitutes a special, unique brand of social signaling. And since conversations happen in real time, involving emotions and fleeting thoughts, many species of punctuation and conventions for emotional nuance are used as substitutions for body language.

4. Text Chat Plus Avatars

This refers to the modes of communication used commonly in Second Life and similar virtual worlds. The user can type text chat in the standard IM way, and also control an avatar similar to the way a character is controlled in a computer game. The user can play avatar animations as a form of body language. The user can also use text to trigger animations. Typically, the avatar is not very much in sync with the expressive dynamics of the text. Consequently, users don't pursue communicative activities that rely on tight synchrony of verbal and nonverbal signals.

5. Voice Chat Plus Avatars

This is similar to the mode above, except the user speaks instead of entering text. This mode may be more natural, but only in the sense that speech is more natural than generating text. There may still be a collision with the 3D avatar if there is no intuitive way to associate avatar gestures with vocal gestures (this is partially addressed with the "voice as puppeteer" mode, coming up).

Increasingly, this mode of communication is combined with text chat. People will often be talking with a group and simultaneously using text chat as a backchannel—such as adding a private comment to one person in the group.

6. Avatar-Centric Communication

This refers to the modes of communication used in virtual worlds such as the interactions afforded in chat props in There.com. It applies a design solution to the collision of text chat and 3D avatar animation by way of chat balloons to give the text embodiment, and allows triggered avatar animations that can be interwoven with text, using a word-at-a-time chat delivery system. It facilitates social gaze that is tied to the chat content. It also employs camera zooms, pans, and cuts to frame social body language and reveal expressions.

7. Voice as Puppeteer

This mode uses the audio signal of the user's voice to create gesticulations in an avatar's head, hands, and upper body. A more sophisticated version would use natural language processing to identify words, meaning, and emotion, and to generate gestural emblems and more sophisticated body language in general. Researchers are currently exploring ways to generate conversational gesture based on verbal language. There is reason to believe that it has great potential, and it may provide a way for automatic and customizable body language to be generated while talking. As discussed in the previous chapter, it captures the gestural origins of speech to reconstitute visual body language.

8. Non-intrusive Partial Motion Capture Plus Voice

This mode uses computer vision. Miniaturized multiple-camera technology is making it easier to track head, eye, and hand motions. This means that a user can move naturally while speaking into a computer or mobile device, and his or her gestures can be detected and applied to an avatar. It would not make as much sense to use this in association with text-chat, because people generally do not create very much communicative body language when they are typing.

9. Full-Body Motion Capture with Voice

This refers to full-body motion capture systems that animate an avatar to accurately replicate the motions of the user. It constitutes a puppeteering system in which the user is tugging at a *maximum* number of puppet strings. And it also represents a short identity leash. This is unlikely to be used much for casual avatar puppeteering since it requires the user to be totally "on" all the time. Because of the shortness of the identity leash, and the maximal number of puppet strings involved, I would place this mode outside of the realm of *avatarhood*.

10. Hybrid of Video Capture and Avatar Animation

Many hybrid forms can be created using combinations of the modes listed above. One that appears to be showing up in various pockets of innovation is the use of video capture not only to drive the motions of an avatar, but also to apply imaging onto the avatar model. For instance, the animated image of the user's face can be mapped to a 3D head. Such systems can also be used to track eye gaze and to reconstitute this in a virtual space. These techniques are highly subject to uncanny valley syndrome, and it may be a while before such avatar systems look and feel natural.

11. Augmented Reality Interfaces

Augmented reality is the application of computer-generated content layered on top of, or altering the view of, the real physical world. Bruce Damer says: "Augmented Reality interfaces and films like *Avatar* are portents of a very different future for avatars in which you will 'walk in' to a projected reality around you in the real world. Think James Cameron holding the virtual camera and walking into an empty warehouse but seeing the completely rendered virtual set with the virtual and actual actors present" (Damer 2010). Augmented reality modes are emerging around us in mobile devices and vehicles. Algorithmic ectoplasm (chat balloons and annotations layered onto real-world scenery) will evolve in this convergence—virtual body language mixed with real body language!

The modalities mentioned above are not the only ones to consider, nor are they equally important as ways to conduct, synthesize, or re-constitute body language remotely. I mention them in order to point out that virtual body language can and will continue to take on many forms. Avatars in virtual worlds are simply one vehicle for doing virtual body language.

Threads

A tangle of email threads has accumulated in my life over the last several decades, and this tangle has become woven into the communicative history of my friends and work partners. Some of that communicative weaving took place face-to-face. I often remember past conversations as if they had happened face-to-face, even though they took place in email form. I imagine the person's voice in my head. I imagine the person's eyes looking at me. Perhaps that is the easiest way for my brain to store those memories, especially as they shift over to long-term memory.

Communication is not only going increasingly online, but it is also being conducted over more kinds of media. Conversational threads can weave through face-to-face conversation, email, instant messaging, Twitter, Facebook, phone, video chat, and in virtual worlds. When a conversational thread is being woven with someone I know extremely well, the various media simply become different views into our conversation, and that person's true identity persists in my memory—much more easily than with a stranger, or someone I have never physically met.

A Future Email Scenario

Given the nature of how our email threads tend to blur in our memory along with the various other media that those threads weave through, imagine now a future form of video-enhanced email that is much more sophisticated, and is able to incorporate some of that memory. Imagine with me the following three communication technologies.

1. Email with Video Attachment

> This refers to the ability for me to record a video of myself talking, and then to add it as an attachment to an email message. The idea is that when you get my email, you will read whatever I have written, and then you will play the video of me talking. You will see and hear my body language. The technology required to do this already exists (e.g., Facebook), but I don't seem to see or hear much about people using this sort of thing. Why? Read on.

2. Email with Video Attachment Plus Video of Recipient's Last Video Message

> Imagine now that am I recording a quick Reply video message to attach to an email message to you. As I am recording myself talking, I am simultaneously watching and listening to the video message that you recorded—which you had attached to your last email to me. Do you think this might give me a feeling of talking to you in realtime? If your answer is "no", you are absolutely correct. In fact, this is about the stupidest thing I can imagine anyone doing. Read on.

3. Email with Video Plus Synthesized Video Based on Previous Videos

> Now let's jump into the future. I crank up your last email, and I start playing the video of you talking to me. I listen to your video message for a while, and then after about 10 seconds of watching and listening, I say, "What? Could you repeat that?" Magically, the video of you talking stops and answers my question…as if you were actually there. Then "you" proceed to continue talking. I nod my head in understanding. Then I cock my head and make a confused face. "You" pause and say, "Do you know what I mean?" I ask you a question and you answer.

We are in full-on conversation mode. But I'm not actually talking to you; I'm talking to a memory of you—an artificial memory that uses our past conversations as a background. This memory is stored in an AI program that is able to reconstitute your body language.

This just might come to pass. Your avatar (or, more like an AI program that knows how you look and move, and has a record of all of our conversations) jumps in and takes over your video messages, and simulates you in a live Skype chat, puppeteering the Skype image and voice all by itself without you having to be there.

Bodymind Mandala

This future scenario takes body language completely out of your own body and generates it in your absence. But is this what you would want? Isn't it best for body language to originate from your own body? That's a fair argument. But I think the boundary of the body is fuzzier than that, and getting fuzzier all the time.

Let's shift our focus up the spinal cord to that overgrown mushroom of neurons: you could also say that body language should originate from your brain (which is part of your body). Viola: *Virtual worlds*. Virtual worlds are manifested in the brain (virtual reality is *all in your mind*). But wait: since the brain is part of the body, virtual worlds are therefore manifest in the body, right? Rather than make a sharp Cartesian distinction between bodily expression and mental expression, consider the whole organism, the social environment, and the various media that amplify and modify expression. Separation of Mind and Body will not help us figure out how to do Virtual Body Language. The key is this: virtual reality is *all in your Bodymind*.

Sandra and Matthew Blakeslee refer to the various body maps in the brain and their exquisite interconnectivity as the "Body Mandala" (2007). The *mandala*—that hypnotic, fractal-like pattern with a concentric circular format, used in Buddhist and Hindu culture for meditation—provides an appropriate metaphor for how our brains integrate the many embodied experiences of our lives...as well as many disembodied experiences. The future of the avatar is pluralistic and multi-faceted, like the Body Mandala. The various forms of virtual body language I have just outlined above hopefully offer a sense of how avatarhood will manifest, become deconstructed, reconstructed, and assimilated into various evolving media.

Jaron Lanier imagines a future of avatar expression in which the avatar's expressive organs can be potentially anything and everything in the virtual world. What if you could wiggle your toes and the clouds moved? The communication homunculus expands to accommodate new bodily expressions, and it could just as easily expand to accommodate clouds. In fact, with the whole virtual environment at your disposal, serving as your *expressive body*, the boundary between *avatar* and *virtual world* essentially vanishes. With the ability to transform yourself into an ice cream cone in order to express your desire to eat ice cream, you have bypassed the symbolic part of language. Lanier calls this "postsymbolic communication" (Lanier, 2010). And so, all this talk about a "body language alphabet" could become quaint – in a future age in which our expression is so fluid, direct, and concrete that there is no longer any need for symbols. Embodied expression will have reached its ultimate state.

On Avatars and Cinnamon Buns

All very cool stuff to think about. But I have to admit, I love what I'm doing right now: chopping away at my laptop in Turk's Coffee House with the smell of coffee and cinnamon buns, the sound of music, and the chatter of busy people around me. They are not distractions; they are part of my creative canvas. Turk's is an exceptionally social café. People of all shapes, sizes, colors, ethnic origins, and nonverbal idiolects come here. There's a guy who dresses up like George Clinton, all clean and wrinkle-free, right before a Funkadelic concert. There is a nun I often see doing paperwork at the corner table. A few disabled people frequent the place: they feel welcome here, and I get to learn a lot about body language while chatting (or gesturing) with them. I have tapped the network, and have gotten to know some of these folks well enough to meet up socially in other places, or to exchange email and web links, and give advice and consolation after a hard day. I love the tingle of face-to-face communication; it generates brain juice: the stuff that flows throughout the bloodstream, throughout the entire body, the stuff that computationalists forget to take into account.

I love hearing people laugh. Sometimes I start laughing with them if their laughter continues on for a while. I don't mind occasionally catching the bodily scent of another person. People are beautiful. The *real* human interface runs at a super high animation frame rate that is not actually an integer. The synchronization of the audio channel with the visual channel is effectively instantaneous, and there is rarely any drop out, unless I've had a few drinks. There is so much to learn from being in the proximity of people in the flesh.

But there is also much to learn from building simulations and playing inside of them. Which is how I ended up writing this book, and it's probably why you are reading it.

In fact, I like to go virtual with my laptop while hanging out at Turks—with the smell of cinnamon buns in the air and the antics of avatars and text threads dancing behind my eyes. I've noticed that shifting back and forth between virtual and real has a kind of intoxicating effect. It's hard to put into words. So I won't bother.

Brains, Bodies, and Future Communication

What does the future hold for avatars? For the sake of argument, consider the following leapfrog-over-the-avatar prediction:

Avatars are fleeting actors in the transitory sputtering of a new communication medium in formation. This new medium will ultimately give way and enable communication that looks and feels like what our ancestors had evolved to do: vocalize, gesticulate, and signal with their whole bodies. Avatars are currently caught up in the tangle of *typewriter ergonomics*.

Take the argument to the extreme. "This too shall pass": pencils, typewriters, avatars—the whole lot. Avatars will dissolve and get mixed into all this transitional media before it dissolves itself into transparency. Avatars, as we know them now, will get shuffled off to the virtual wax museums. We will return to direct physical expression. Our body language will be directly converted into electrical patterns and distributed around the world within seconds. The internet will become a neo-neocortex, strewn with virtual homunculi. New technologies for conducting natural language over the internet will become so invisible and natural that we won't even know it's there.

Agree or disagree?

Think of telephones. When I was a kid, talking on the phone was synonymous with holding a large dumbbell-shaped object to your head which was tethered to the wall by a thick umbilical cord. In those days, it would be absurd to call someone and ask, "Where are you?" I have experienced the nearly-invisible effect of a Bluetooth device on my ear—leaving my hands free to gesticulate, or work a stir-fry. Maybe telephony will become even more invisible, going deeper into the ear, closer to the brain. Maybe my Skype calls will just be wired into my brain, tapping hippocampus, insula, and parietal lobe, requiring only tiny bursts of well-timed electrical patterning to evoke the reality of my wife's expressions and my responses.

Scared yet?

One final question: Why would you want to use a synthetic animated character when you can just be yourself? I have four answers to this question:

(1) We don't always want to be *ourselves*.
(2) Communication/expression is not necessarily better when it is conducted in human form.
(3) Communication/expression sometimes yearns to become *artifact*, external to brain and body.
(4) Human expression is so beautiful and complex and deep that we often need more than these ancient old physical bodies to create it.

Thus, avatars, in the most general sense, will never go extinct. Avatars may be fumbling media-mash hybrids, causing virtual faux pas, but they are also really, really *cool*. And they permit us to craft all kinds of body language—at a distance. They are our digital puppets. We do so love our puppets!

Appendix: A Manifesto of Avatar Expression

(published online at www.avatarexpression.com)

1. Outer Your Inner Avatar

"Avatar", from Hindu mythology, is Sanskrit for "descent" (from heaven to earth). It is a deliberate descent—a purposeful manifestation. "Avatar" is also the embodied *nonverbal communication locus on the internet.*

2. Keep your Body

Technology can be used as a way to become more *Human*, rather than more *Machine*. Subvert technology to the laws of Human Nature. If you are confused because human nature is a moving target, look to our earthly ancestors for inspiration and grounding. We are shifting between animal and post-human. We must not abandon our animal origins.

3. Behavioral Realism is Key

 The concept of "Realism" is still heavily influenced by references to High Renaissance painting. Visual, optical, perspective realism does not contribute to communication in virtual worlds, and in fact, it may detract. *Behavioral Realism* is the key. *Realism* in virtual worlds is tied to *believability* (as it is in fiction). It is not a computer graphic rendering problem. It is a Human Computer-Interaction problem.

4. Own Your Body Language

 A virtual world company may have a financial bottom-line, an ideology, or a business agenda. And the shareholders may not share, or hold, your values. Own your own expression in these virtual worlds. If your avatar generates a nonverbal lie, make sure it is **your** lie. If you cannot generate your own nonverbal lie, or if your lie is generated within the virtual world without your consent, switch to another virtual world that supports user-created content. User-generated content is an important part of internet life. And the most important kind of user-generated content is your own expression.

5. Promote Physical Health Through Technology

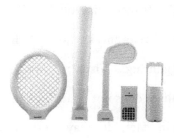

If you are a software developer, educator, web designer, hardware engineer, or business entrepreneur, help find ways to accelerate more innovations like the Wii device. These kinds of interfaces can help reduce childhood obesity and diabetes.

6. Promote a Mathematics of Social Connectedness

Maximally-social virtual body language means seamless translation between the local (personal) coordinate system and the global (social) coordinate system. Mathematically-speaking, that means having software interfaces to transform the local geometry of the body to the global geometry of the world. Without this translation, we have unresponsive, socially-inept avatars. This is a simulation methodology that ultimately impacts virtual embodied communication.

7. Humanize Technology

Those of us with roots in the humanities and arts must embrace software technology, harness it, and loosen the grip of a left-brain dominated software culture. Computing is not about numbers. It is about intuition, knowledge sharing, and Intelligence Amplification (IA, not just AI). If you are an artist, boldly engage the software world. Use whatever strategies you have available to make software less machine, more **human**.

8. Foster Global Affective Communication

Virtual Body Language is not an Ivory Tower academic subject. It is part of our future (and present). We have an opportunity to build the foundations of deep affective communication over the internet, to foster understanding and intercultural communication in the global village.

References

Allbeck, J. and Badler, N. 2003. "Representing and Parameterizing Agent Behaviors". *Life-like Characters: Tools, Affective Functions and Applications*. Helmut Prendinger and Mitsuru Ishizuka, Ed. Springer, Germany.

Au, Wagner James. 2006. "The Uncanny Valley Expo". New World Notes blog: http://nwn.blogs.com/nwn/2006/08/the_uncanny_val.html.

Badler, N., et al. 1991. *Making Them Move*. Morgan Kauffman.

Bailenson, J., et al. 2005. "The independent and interactive effects of embodied-agent appearance and behavior on self-report, cognitive, and behavioral markers of copresence in immersive virtual environments". *Presence: Teleoperators and Virtual Environments*. Volume 14, Issue 4. MIT Press.

Bartle, R. 2004. *Designing Virtual Worlds*. New Riders Publishing.

Bates, B., and Cleese, J. 2001. *The Human Face*. BBC Worldwide Limited.

Beattie, G. 2003. *Visible Thought: The New Psychology Of Body Language*. Routledge.

Birdwhistell, R. 1970. *Kinesics and Context*. University of Pennsylvania Press.

Bizzocchi, J. 2011. (personal communication)

Blakeslee, S., and Blakeslee, M. 2007. *The Body Has a Mind of its Own*. Random House.

Boellstorff, T. 2010. "Culture of the Cloud". *Journal of Virtual Worlds Research: The Metaverse Assembled*. Volume 2, No 5. May, 2010.

Brooks, R. "Elephants Don't Play Chess". 1990. *Robotics and Autonomous Systems*. Volume 6, Numbers 1&2, Pages 3-15.

Cameron, J. 2009. Interview with Discovery Channel, available on YouTube, Avatar: Motion Capture Mirrors Emotions, December, 24, 2009. http://www.youtube.com/watch?v=1wK1Ixr-UmM.

Cardenas, M. 2010. quote from a personal video chat interview about *Becoming Dragon*, May, 2010.

Carr, N. 2010. *The Shallows: What the Internet is Doing to our Brains*. W.W. Norton and Company.

Cassell, J. 2001. "Embodied Conversational Agents: Representation and Intelligence in User Interfaces," *AI Magazine*, vol. 22.

Chippendale, P. 2006. "Towards Automatic Body Language Annotation". pp.487-492, Seventh IEEE International Conference on Automatic Face and Gesture Recognition (FG'06).

Clanton, C., Ventrella, J. 2003. Avatar-centric Communication in There. Presentation at the People, Computers and Design seminar, Stanford University. http://hci.stanford.edu/courses/cs547/abstracts/02-03/030404-clanton.html.

Damer, B. 1998. *Avatars! Exploring and Building Virtual Worlds on the Internet*. Peachpit Press.

Damer, B. 2010. personal email correspondence. January, 2010.

Deacon, T. 1997. *The Symbolic Species: The Co-evolution of Language and the Brain*. New York, Norton.

de Andrade, N.N.G. 2009. "Striking a Balance between Property and Personality: The Case of the Avatars". *Journal of Virtual Worlds Research*, Volume 1, Number 3. http://journals.tdl.org/jvwr/article/viewArticle/362.

deGraf, B., and Yilmaz, E. 1999. "Puppetology: Science or Cult?" *Animation World Magazine*, issue 3.11 – February 1999.

DiPaola S, Turner J. 2008. "Authoring the Intimate Self: Identity, Expression and Role-playing within a Pioneering Virtual Community". Journal of the Canadian Games Studies Association, Vol 1, No 3

DiPaola, S. 2000. Notes from the Siggraph 2000 Panel on Interactive Storytelling.

Doidge, Normon. 2007. *The Brain that Changes Itself*. James H. Silberman Books.

Donath, J. 2010. "A Reflection on Jeremy Bailenson's talk", from the following web site: http://blogs.law.harvard.edu/lawlab/2010/02/10/a-reflection-on-jeremy-bailenson's-talk-from-judith-donath/.

Dreyfus, H. 1972. *What Computers Can't Do – The Limits of Artificial Intelligence*. MIT Press.

Ekman, P., Friesen, W., and Bear, J. 1984. "The International Language of Gestures". *Psychology Today* 18. p64-69.

Engage Digital. 2009. Virtual World Popularity Spikes. Blog: http://www.engagedigital.com/2009/07/15/virtual-world-popularity-spikes/

Fast, Julius. 1971. *Body Language*. Pocket Books.

Ferrer i Cancho, R. and Lusseau, D. 2009. "Efficient coding in dolphin surface behavioral patterns". *Complexity* 14 (5): 23-25.

French, R. 2009. "If it walks like a duck and quacks like a duck... The Turing Test, Intelligence and Consciousness". *Oxford Companion to Consciousness*. Wilken, Bayne, Cleeremans (eds.) Oxford Univ. Press. 461-463.

Freud, S. 1919. "Das Unheimliche" (The Uncanny).

Gajadhar, J., and Green, J. 2005. "The Importance of Nonverbal Elements in Online Chat". *Educause Quarterly*, number 4.

Gauthier, I., Curran, T., Curby, K.M. & Collins, D. 2003. "Perceptual interference supports a non-modular account of face processing." *Nature Neuroscience*, 6 (4),428-432.

Gemmell, J., Zitnick, L. C., Kang, T., Toyama, K., and Seitz, S. 2000. "Gaze awareness for video-conferencing: a software approach". *Multimedia*, Volume 7, Issue 4. pp 26-35. IEEE.

Gould, S. and Vrba, E. S. 1982. "Exaptation — a missing term in the science of form" *Paleobiology* 8 (1): 4–15.

Gould, S. 1993. Looney Tuniverse: "There is a crazy king of physics at work in the world of cartoons". *New Scientist*.

Grandin, T., and Johnson, C. 2005. "Animals emotion is simple and pure; Similarities between animal and autistic emotion". *Animals in Translation*. New York: Scribner.

Gratch, J., Wang, N., Okhmatovskaia A., Lamothe, F., Morales, M., R., van der Werf R. J., and Morency, L. P. 2007. "Can virtual humans be more engaging than real ones?" *Human-Computer Interaction. HCI Intelligent Multimodal Interaction Environments*. Springer, 2007.

Hafting T., Fyhn M., Molden S., Moser M. B., Moser E. I. 2005. "Microstructure of a spatial map in the entorhinal cortex". *Nature*. Aug 11, 2005.

Hayles, K. 1999. *How We Became Posthuman: Virtual Bodies in Cybernetics, Literature, and Informatics*. University of Chicago Press.

Heim, M. 2001. "The avatar and the power grid". *Mots Pluriels*, No. 19. October 2001. http://www.arts.uwa.edu.au/MotsPluriels/MP1901mh.html.

Hewes, Gordon W. 1973 . "Primate communication and the gestural origins of language". *Current Anthropology* 14:5-24. 1973.

Hooks, E. 2003. *Acting for Animators*. Heinemann

Isbister, K. 2004 ."Building Bridges Through the Unspoken: Embodied Agents to Facilitate Intercultural Communication". *Agent culture: human-agent interaction in a multicultural World*, by Payr, R., and Trappl, R. (editors). CRC Press.

Isbister, K., Seif El-Nasr, M., and Ventrella, J. 2010. "Avatars with Improved Social Signaling." *CHI 2010 Workshop on Designing and Evaluating Affective Aspects of Sociable Media to Support Social Connectedness*.

Isbister, K. 2006. *Better Game Characters by Design: A Psychological Approach*. Elsevier.

Iverson, J. M., Tencer, H. L., Lany, J. and Goldin-Meadow, S. 2000. "The Relation Between Gesture and Speech in Congenitally Blind and Sighted Language-Learners." *Journal of Nonverbal Behavior*. vol 24. Number 2. Springer.

Jenkins, H. 2010. Interviewed on Frontline: "Digital_Nation: Life on the Virtual Frontier". February, 2010. http://www.pbs.org/wgbh/pages/frontline/digitalnation/virtual-worlds/second-lives/the-human-behind-the-avatar.html?play.

Jones, C. 1989. Chuck Amuck – The Life and Times of an Animated Cartoonist. Farrar, Straus and Giroux. Page 13.

Kastleman, M. 2001. *The Drug of the New Millennium: The Science of How Internet Pornography Radically Alters the Human Brain and Body*. Granite.

Kellert, S. R., and Wilson, E. O. 1993. *The Biophilia Hypothesis*. Island Press.

Kendon, A. 2004. *Gesture: Visible Action as Utterance*. Cambridge University Press.

Kipp, M., Neff, M., and Albrecht, I. 2007. "An Annotation Scheme for Conversational Gestures: How to Economically Capture Timing and Form." *Journal on Language Resources and Evaluation*. Volume 47, Numbers 3-4. 2007. Springer.

Kopp, S., Krenn, B., Marsella, S., Marshall, A. N., Pelachaud, C., Pirker, H., Thórisson, K. R., and Vilhjálmsson H. 2006. "Towards a Common Framework for Multimodal Generation: The Behavior Markup Language". *Lecture Notes in Computer Science*. Springer Volume 4133.

Koster, R. "Avatar Body Language" – published in *Raph Koster's Website*. June 8, 2009. http://www.raphkoster.com/2009/06/08/avatar-body-language.

Kurlander, D., Skelly, T., Salesin, D. 1996. "Comic Chat". *Proceedings of SIGGRAPH '96*. pp. 225-236. August 1996.

Kurzweil, R. 2005. *The Singularity is Near – When Humans Transcend Biology*. Viking.

Lance, B., and Marcella, S. 2010. "Glances, glares, and glowering: how should a virtual human express emotion through gaze?" *Autonomous Agents and Multi-Agent Systems*, Volume 20, number 1. Springer.

Lanier, J. 2006. "What cephalopods can teach us about language". *Discover*. April 2, 2006.

Lanier, J. 2010. You Are Not a Gadget – A Manifesto. Vintage Books.

Lavenac, E. 2007. YouTube video: *Second Life*. Draftfcb/paris:
http://www.youtube.com/watch?v=flkgNn50k14 .

Linden Lab. 2009. "Puppeteering" *Second Life Wiki*:
http://wiki.secondlife.com/wiki/Puppeteering. Also described in
www.avatarpuppeteering.com

Livingstone, D. 2006. "Turing's Test and Believable AI in Games." *Computers in
Entertainment*. Volume 4, Issue 1.

Mania, K. and Chalmers, A. 1998. "A Classification for User Embodiment in
Collaborative Virtual Environments". *Proceedings of the 4th International
Conference on Virtual Systems and Multimedia*. IOS Press. pp. 177–182.

Maturana, H. R. and Varela, F. J. 1992. *The Tree of Knowledge – The Biological
Roots of Human Understanding*. Shambhala.

McCloud, S. 1993. *Understanding Comics, The Invisible Art*. Tundra Publishing.

McNeill, D. 1996. *Hand and Mind: What Gestures Reveal About Thought*.
University of Chicago Press.

McNeill, D. 1998. *The Face*. Little, Brown and Company.

Meadows, M. S. 2008. *I Avatar: The Culture and Consequences of Having a Second
Life*. New Riders.

Moore, R. J. 2009. Personal communications: email interview.

Müller, R., Pannasch, S., Velichkovsky, B. M. 2009. "Comparing eye
movements for perception and communication: Changes in visual
fixation durations and saccadic amplitudes". *Perception* 38 ECVP
Abstract Supplement, page 23.

Murray, C. D., Pettifer S., Howard T., Patchick E. L., Caillette F., Kulkarni
J., Bamford C. 2007. "The treatment of phantom limb pain using immersive
virtual reality: three case studies". *Disability and rehabilitation*. vol 29 (issue
18) : pp 1465-9.

Nassiri, N., Powell, N., and Moore, D. 2004. "Avatar gender and personal space
invasion anxiety level in desktop collaborative virtual environments".
Virtual Reality. Volume 8, Number 2. Springer.

Neff, M. Kipp, M., Albrecht., I., and Seidel, H. 2008. "Gesture Modeling and Animation Based on Probabilistic Recreation of Speaker Style". *ACM Transactions on Graphics*. vol. 27. Issue 1, March.

Nelson, T. 2008. *Geeks Bearing Gifts: How the Computer World Got This Way.* Mindful Press.

Norman, D. 1992. *Turn Signals are the Facial Expressions of Cars.* Addison-Wesley.

O'Donnell, M. 1980. "O'Donnell's Laws of Cartoon Motion". *Esquire.* June, 1980.

O'Keefe, J., and Dostrovsky, J. 1971. "The hippocampus as a spatial map. Preliminary evidence from unit activity in the freely-moving rat" in *Brain Research* Volume 34, pages 171-175.

Pearce, C. 2009. *Communities of Play – Emergent Cultures in Multiplayer Games and Virtual Worlds.* MIT Press.

Pentland, Alex (Sandy). 2008. *Honest Signals.* MIT Press.

Perlin, K. 1995. "Real Time Responsive Animation with Personality". *IEEE Transactions on Visualization and Computer Graphics.* Volume 1, Issue 1, March, 1995.

Persson, P. 2003. "ExMS: an Animated and Avatar-based Messaging System for Expressive Peer Communication". *Proceedings of GROUP 2003 conference,* Nov. 9-12, 2003.

Quaranta, A., Siniscalchi, M., Vallortigara, G. 2007. "Asymmetric tail-wagging responses by dogs to different emotive stimuli". *Current Biology,* Volume 17 , Issue 6 , Pages R199 - R201.

Rist, T., Pelachaud, C., and Krenn, B. 2003. *Wrap-up and Conclusions from the Vienna Gesticon Workshop.* http://www.ofai.at/research/nlu/NECA/GesticonsWS/gesticon_wrap-upv3.pdf.

Roberts, D. et al. 2009. "Communicating Eye-gaze Across a Distance: Comparing an Eye-gaze enabled Immersive Collaborative Virtual Environment, Aligned Video Conferencing, and Being Together". *IEEE Virtual Reality* 2009, p.p. 135-142.

Rotman, B. 2008. *Becoming Beside Ourselves: The Alphabet, Ghosts, and Distributed Human Being*. Duke University Press.

Salem, B. Earle, N. 2000. "Designing a non-verbal language for expressive avatars". *Proceedings of the Third International Conference on Collaborative Virtual Environments*. ACM.

Sarcmark.com (web site with advertisement for the sarcmark punctuation mark: http://www.sarcmark.com).

Schrödinger, E. "What is Life?" 1944. *Cambridge University Press*.

Schroeder, R. (editor). 2002. *The Social Life of Avatars: Presence and Interaction in Shared Virtual Environments*. Springer Verlag.

Seif El-Nasr, M., Isbister, K., Ventrella, J., Aghabeigi, B., Hash, C., Morie, J., Bishko, L. 2011. "Body Buddies: Social Signaling through Pupeteering." proceedings of HCI International.

Seif El-Nasr, M., Bishko, L., Zammitto, V, Nixon, M., and Athanasios, V. 2009. "Believable Characters". *Handbook of Digital Media in Entertainment and Arts*. chapter 22. Furht, B. (editor). Springer.

Sheridan, M.D. 1977. "Observations on the development of spontaneous tele-kinesic communication in babies and young children". *Child Care Health Development*. May 1977. (Vol. 3, Issue 3, Pages 189-99).

Stephenson, N. 1992. *Snow Crash*. Bantam Books. Page 60.

Stevens, T. 2006. quoted in Wikipedia: http://en.wikipedia.org/wiki/Series_of_tubes.

Suler, John. The Psychology of CyberSpace. A hypertext book online at: http://www-usr.rider.edu/~suler/psycyber/psycyber.html Department of Psychology, Science and Technology Center, Rider University.

Tashian, C. 2000. "Lost in Translation": a web site for multi-language translation, causing babbled text: tashian.com/multibabel/.

Tromp, J, and Snowdon, D. 1997. "Virtual Body Language: providing appropriate user interfaces in collaborative virtual environments". *Proceedings of the ACM symposium on virtual reality software and technology*. Pages 37-44. ACM.

Truss, L. 2003. Eats, *Shoots and Leaves*. Gotham Books.

Tufte, E. R. 1990. *Envisioning Information*. Graphics Press.

Tufte, E. R. 2006. *Beautiful Evidence*. Graphics Press.

Turing, A. M. 1950. "Computing Machinery and Intelligence". *Mind*.

Turkle, S. 1995. *Life on the Screen*. Touchstone.

van Welbergen, H., Ruttkay, Z., and Varga , B. 2008. "Informed Use of Motion Synthesis Methods". *Motion in Games*. Springer.

Ventrella, J., Seif El-Nasr, M., Aghabeigi, A., Overington, R. 2010. "Gestural Turing Test: A Motion-Capture Experiment for Exploring Nonverbal Communication". AAMAS 2010, International Workshop on Interacting with ECA's as Virtual Characters. http://www.gesturalturingtest.com/

Verhulsdonck, G., 2007. "Issues of designing gestures into online interactions: implications for communicating in virtual environments". *Proceesdings of SIGDOC '07*. ACM.

Verhulsdonck, G., and Morie, J. F. 2009. "Virtual Chironomia: Developing Non-verbal Communication Standards in Virtual Worlds". *Journal of Virtual Worlds Research*. Volume 2, number 3. October, 2009.

Vesna, V. 2004. "Community of People with No Time: Collaboration Shifts". *First Person: New Media as Story, Performance, and Game*. Ed. Wardrip-Fruin, N., Harrigan, P. MIT Press.

von Károlyi, C., Winner, E., Gray, W., and Sherman, G. F. 2003. "Dyslexia linked to talent: Global visual-spatial ability". *Brain and Language*. Volume 85, Issue 3, June 2003, Pages 427-431.

Watters, A. 2010. "Number of Virtual World Users Breaks 1 Billion, Roughly Half Under Age 15". From the blog: Read Write Web. http://www.readwriteweb.com/archives/number_of_virtual_world_u sers_breaks_the_1_billion.php

White, M. "Visual Pleasure in Textual Places: Gazing in multi-user object-oriented worlds". *Information, Communication & Society*. Volume 2, Issue 4. December, 2001. Pages 496-520.

Wilson, E. O. 1975. *Sociobiology*. Harvard College.

Wilson, F. R. 1998. *The Hand – How its use shapes the brain, language, and human culture*. Vintage Books.

Woita, S. 2010. personal communication.
  http://www.linkedin.com/in/susanwoita.

Yakal, K. 1986. "A Look at the Future of Online Games". *Compute!* Issue 77,
  October 1986. Page 32.

Yee, N., Ellis, J., Ducheneaut, N. 2009. "The Tyranny of Embodiment". *Artifact*,
  Vol. 2, 2009, 1-6.

Yee, N. 2007. "The Proteus Effect: Behavioral Modification via Transformations
  of Digital Self-Representation": Stanford University Ph.D. dissertation.

Yip, B. and Jin, J.S. 2003. "An effective eye gaze correction operation for video
  conference using antirotation formulas". *Information, Communications and
  Signal Processing, 2003 and the Fourth Pacific Rim Conference on Multimedia*.

ABOUT THE AUTHOR

Jeffrey Ventrella is an artist and software programmer. He writes about artificial life, virtual worlds, and computer art, and has lectured in North America and Europe. He is a graduate of the MIT Media Lab, and the co-founder of the now-defunct virtual world, There.com. He invented the flexiprims of Second Life. Ventrella created *GenePool*, an artificial life game, and other interactive animations, available on www.ventrella.com. He lives in northern California with his wife Nuala and his dog Higgs.

RELATED WEBSITES BY THE AUTHOR

www.avatarpuppeteering.com

www.avatarexpression.com

www.avatology.com

www.birthofthere.com

www.gesturalturingtest.com

www.ventrella.com

Index

Aberdeen University, 160

Abraham Lincoln, 66

Accelerometer, 26

Acting, 31, 42, 148, 214, 218, 223

Active Worlds, 239

Aesthetics, 154

Affectations, 26

Affective, 32, 261

Affordances, 14, 138

African music, 112

Aghabeigi, Bardia, 133

Alphabetic Body, 113

Alphaworld, 164

Analog, 98, 99, 111, 112, 114, 181, 232

Analytic Cubism, 201

Anatomy, 130, 137, 150, 153

Animal, 35, 47, 124, 144, 145, 153, 155, 216, 258, 265

Animated character, 111, 257

Animator, 40, 96, 147, 191

Anorexia, 146

Anthropomorphism, 145, 146

Aphex Twin, 112

Apple, 44

Armstrong, Louis, 122

Art of Body Language, 39

Artandi, Stacey, 30

Articulation, 68

Artificial intelligence, 81, 125, 220

Artificial Reality, 95

ASCII, 110

Asynchronous communication, 14

Authenticity, 41

Autism, 18, 33, 142

Autonomic, 216

Autonomous agents, 208

Avatar animation, 17, 91, 94, 152, 209, 233, 237, 248

Avatar body language, 31, 32, 58, 106

Avatar breathing, 216

Avatar customization, 94, 188

Avatar design, 33, 89, 119

Avatar expression, 18, 21, 41, 72, 74, 119, 174, 233, 254

Avatar gaze, 78, 90, 185, 187, 194, 202

Avatar hands, 152

Avatar puppeteering, 88, 223, 229, 249

Avatar skeleton, 70, 145, 222

Avatar-Centric Communication, 56, 72, 74-76, 78, 85, 89, 91, 93, 168, 186, 248

Away From Keyboard, 85

Babel Fish, 27, 28

Babelizer, 28

Bachleitner, Anton, 214

Backchannel, 248

Badler, Norm, 31, 98, 189, 215, 262

Bailenson, Jeremy, 42, 121, 146, 262, 264

Bandwidth, 32, 97, 101, 107

Bar-Yam, Yaneer, 119

Bartle, Richard, 73, 262

Bates, Brian, 20

BBC, 20, 262

Beattie, Geoffrey, 40

Becoming Dragon, 148, 263

Beecher, Henry Ward, 37

Beethoven, 96

Behavior Markup Language, 98, 266

Behavioral realism, 31, 119, 120, 121, 123, 130

Believability, 121, 123, 124, 130, 131, 133, 135, 136, 206, 259

Bierce, Ambrose, 48

Biology, 33, 35, 48

Biophilia, 139, 266

Bipedal, 58, 212

Birdwhistell, Ray, 19, 23, 109, 262

Bit Torrent, 106

Black Sun, 33

Blakeslee, Sandra and Matthew, 193, 208, 254, 262

Bluetooth, 256

Blumberg, Bruce, 156

Bodily Contact, 93

Body gaze, 83

Body image, 146, 147, 149

Body language alphabet, 22, 94, 98, 109, 110, 114, 153, 161, 254

Body Mandala, 254

Body map, 94, 208, 215

Body schema, 193, 212, 215

Bodymind, 97, 253

Boellstorff, Tom, 14, 262

Boolean, 102, 157, 159

Botticelli, 182

BPPV, 63

Brain disorders, 146

BRB, 85

Brooks, Rodney, 126

Bumgardner, Jim, 10, 82

Caching, 104

Calvert, Tom, 215

Cameron, James, 123, 250, 262

Car, 47

Cardenas, Micha, 148, 149, 154, 263

Carlin, George, 28

Cartoon, 45, 70, 147, 150, 154, 156

Cassell, Justine, 127

Cat, 123, 143, 155, 186

Cephalopods, 159, 161, 266

Cerebellum, 33, 206, 208, 212

Chalmers, A., 93, 267

Character animation, 68-70, 138, 147, 215, 228

Chat balloons, 74, 162-165, 175, 176

Chat Group, 168

Chat props, 82, 84, 248

Chemical, 34, 35

Chimpanzees, 231

Choreography, 113, 234

Cinematographer, 79

Circumflex Accent, 48

Clanton, Chuck, 74, 152, 173, 263

Cleese, John, 20

Clippy, 51

Cloud, the, 14

Cohen, Bram, 106

Collaborative virtual environments, 127, 267, 269

Comic Chat, 165, 166, 266

Communities of Play, 90, 268

Complexity, 32, 97, 103, 222

Computer games, 14, 31, 79, 81, 94, 100, 127, 216

Computer graphics, 62, 115, 119, 120, 152, 211

Computer-Mediated Communication, 73

Continuous Partial Attention, 9

Contrapposto, 218

Conversation Circles, 76

Copresence, 9, 73, 121, 262

Coverbal, 229

Creativity, 42, 227

Cuttlefish, 159, 160

Cybertown, 12

Cylinder, 57-59, 63, 91

Damer, Bruce, 27, 61, 250, 263

Darwinian, 38

Data compression, 102

Deep Blue, 126

deGraf, Brad, 20, 147, 148, 263

Deictics, 110

Deacon, Terrence, 232

Descartes, Rene, 208

Dick Tracy, 103

Digital puppets, 122, 123, 257

Digital Space Traveler, 61

DiPaola, Steve, 10, 62, 90, 238, 263

Direct manipulation, 223

Directly-captured, 95, 98, 103

Disabled, 22, 96, 97, 255

Discrete, 112, 113, 160

DNA, 23, 145

Donath, Judith, 42, 244

Dog body language, 141, 143

Dogz, 156

Dolphins, 159

Dreyfus, Hubert, 126

Ducheneaut, Nic, 117, 118, 271

Duchenne smile, 45

Duckling, 212-214

Duda, Ken, 76

Dyslexia, 270

Ears, 23, 103, 140-143, 146, 156, 157, 162

Earth, 24, 34, 92, 211

Eco, Umberto, 41

Ectoplasm, 78, 162

Education, 20, 41, 75

Ekman, Paul, 41, 98, 109, 264

Electromagnetic, 103

Elephants, 126, 262

Email, 14, 21, 50, 126, 251, 252, 255, 263, 267

Emblems, 110, 132, 240, 249

Embodied communication, 13, 24, 73, 78, 91, 175, 260

Embodied conversational agents, 98, 189

Emily Carr University, 133, 135

Emily Project, 122

Emoticon, 21, 48, 50, 52

Encoded body language, 95-97, 99, 100

Endorphin, 207

Endosymbiotic theory, 48

English, 28, 110

Entropy, 210

Epilepsy, 150

Epley maneuver, 63

Esperanto, 28

Euphoria, 207

Exaptation, 49, 264

Expressivity, 22, 69, 70, 74, 97, 119, 227, 229

Eye contact, 18, 140, 141, 176, 180, 218

Eye gaze, 70, 182, 190, 250, 271

Eye tracking, 189

Eyeball, 69, 181, 184

Eyeball rotations, 70

Eyeballs, 69, 123, 154, 181, 184

Eye-brain, 46, 117, 185

Eyebrows, 48, 71, 140, 180, 235, 237, 238

Eyelids, 69, 109

Facebook, 14, 47, 251, 252

Face-to-face, 20, 25, 26, 42, 49, 251, 255

Facial Action Coding System, 98

Facial animation, 45, 122, 235, 236, 237

Facial expression, 16, 18, 24, 27, 33, 36, 46, 83, 93, 114, 174, 234, 238, 240, 245

Fahlman, Scott, 48

Farmer, Randy, 17

Fast, Julius, 39

Faux pas, 9, 14, 257

First person, 61, 197, 198

Flat-shading, 236

Flirting, 83

Freud, Sigmund, 116

Friesen, Wallace, 98, 109, 264

Frisbee, 156

Frontline, 20, 266

Fulop, Rob, 156

Furry, 43, 144, 145, 146

Galileo, 47, 52

Gayeton, Douglas, 237

Gaze Vector, 177, 179, 183

Gender, 149, 267

Genetics, 119, 120

Gesticon, 98, 268

Gesticulation, 17, 87, 99, 233, 235, 239, 242

Gestionary, 98

Gestural Theory, 38, 39, 231, 232

Gesture, 19, 34, 38, 39, 52, 93, 98, 111, 173, 218, 219, 232, 233, 243, 247, 249

Gesture Recognition, 263

Goffman, Erving, 10

Golem, 214

Gould, Stephen Jay, 49

Graded signals, 112

Grandin, Temple, 142

Gratch, Jonathan, 41, 265

Griefing, 94

Habitat, 17, 164

Hand gestures, 16, 18, 236, 242

Harvey, Will, 56, 63, 64

Hayles, N. Katherine, 126

Head motion, 185

Head orientation, 63, 140

Head rotation, 58, 185, 189, 199

Head waggle, 222

Head-mounted displays, 146, 199

Heads Up Display, 177

Heim, Michael, 54

Hierarchical animation, 225, 226

Hierarchical modeling, 68, 69, 215

Hierarchical Puppetry, 214

Hiro Protagonist, 32

Holding hands, 71

Homo Sapiens, 38, 44, 142, 144, 159

Homunculus, 150

Honest Signals, 19, 26, 268

Hooke's Law, 223

Hox genes, 145

Human communication, 19, 35, 38, 105, 157

Human-Computer Interaction, 74, 265

Humanoid, 100, 101, 124

Hyperlink, 52, 53

Hyperlinks, 52

Hyper-Realism, 121

Iconics, 110

Identity, 10, 11, 14, 47, 88, 123, 149, 241, 249, 251

Identity leash, 10, 250

Idiolect, 242-245

Image Metrics, 122

Imitation, 129, 135, 137

Immersive, 146, 201, 268

IMVU, 217

Indian, 63, 222

Inflatable Wavers, 220

Inner ear, 58, 62, 63, 64

Instant messaging, 9, 12, 73, 76, 126, 173, 247, 251

Intelligence Amplification, 261

Interactive Art, vi, 133

Invasion anxiety, 61, 267

Inverse-kinematics, 66, 191, 204, 215, 226

iPad, 44, 229

iPhone, 28

Isbister, Katherine, 29

Iverson, Jana, 39

Jabba the Hut, 234

Jake Sully, 88

Jenkins, Henry, 20

Joint rotation, 191

Jones, Chuck, 117

Juanita Marquez, 32

Kahle, Brewster, 28

Kasparov, Garry, 126

Kataspace, 191

Kellert, S. R., 139, 266

Kendon, Adam, 19

Keyframes, 228

Kinect, 241

Kinesics, 19, 23, 109

Kipp, Michael, 111, 266, 268

Kissing, 199

Kopp, S., 98, 266

Koster, Raph, 32, 266

Krueger, Myron, 95

Kurzweil, Ray, 105

Laban, Rudolf, 113

Lanier, Jaron, 159, 160, 254, 266, 267

Lara Croft, 31, 33

Legoues, Francoise, 25

Leonardo, 47, 52

Library of Babel, 106

Lie To Me, 41

Limbic system, 25, 33, 102, 212

Linden Lab, 8, 74, 87, 145, 222, 223, 229, 267

Lipreading, 235

Lips, 16, 71, 113, 123, 150, 233, 235, 236, 237, 238

Lip-sync, 233-235, 237

Locomotion, 47, 65, 154, 231

LOL, 52

Lookat, 8, 78, 89

Love Seat, 83

LSL, 145

Lucasfilm, 17

Lying, 27, 41, 42, 55, 88

Marcella, S., 189, 266

Magnenat-Thalmann, Nadia, 115, 119

Mario, 33, 64, 66

Marionette, 206, 212-214

Massey, Colm, 207

Maturana, H.R., 108, 267

Meadows, Mark Stephen, 47

Melcher, Tom, 72

McCloud, Scott, 10, 117

McLuhan, Marshall, 47

McNeill, Daniel, 45, 110, 267

Media Lab, 42, 107, 156, 272

Memes, 74, 103

Message-passing, 93, 159

Metaverse, 33, 262

Michelangelo, 127, 151

Micro-expressions, 183

Microgestures, 109

Microphone, 16, 26, 202, 239

Microsoft, 50, 51, 165, 166, 241

Minsky, Marvin, 208

MIRALab, 115

Mirror neurons, 137, 193

Mirroring, 136, 137

Molotov Alva, 237

Monroe, Marilyn, 115, 119

Moodicons, 13, 83, 93

Moore, Bob, 173

Morency, Louis-Philippe, 189, 265

Mori, Masahiro, 116

Morie, Jackie, 14, 269, 270

Morningstar, Chip, 17

Moswitzer, Max, 154

Motion-Capture, 241, 270

Mouse cursor, 33, 53, 78, 186, 222, 224, 225

Mouth, 44, 45, 140, 150, 231, 233-235, 237, 238, 239

Multihomuncular, 160

Multimodal, 34, 78, 98, 236

Multi-user-dungeon, 73

Muscles, 16, 45, 46, 140, 143, 144, 209, 214, 215

Na'vi, 88, 123, 237

Nabokov, V. 48

Narrative, 48, 87, 197, 234, 238

Natural language, 18, 23, 43, 98, 129, 160, 165, 173, 183, 232, 240, 249, 256

NaturalMotion, 207, 208

Neff, Michael, 242, 243, 266, 268

Negroponte, Nicholas, 107

Nelson, Richard, 185

Nelson, Ted, 15

Neural Plasticity, 139

Neuroscience, 208

Newtonian Physics, 65

Nodding, 63, 228

Non-human, 68, 117, 124, 145, 148, 153, 155, 236

Non-symbolic media, 95

Nonverbal communication, 14, 18, 19, 29, 60, 91, 99, 150, 163, 218, 246, 258

Nonverbal expression, 18, 21, 22, 29, 48, 110, 174, 206

Norman, Donald, 140

Nose, 44, 59, 109, 119

Notational media, 95, 113

Nystagmus, 63

Oculomotor, 181

Online chat, 49

Onlive Traveler, 61, 62

Onomatopoeia, 49

Out-of-body, 22, 148

Overington, Rick, 134

Owen Turner, Jeremy, 13, 86, 154

Oxford, 207, 264

PacMan, 33, 100, 217

Palace, the, 10, 82, 164

Paralanguage, 19

Parameterized Action
    Representation, 98

Pearce, Celia, 90, 268

Penfield, Wilder, 150

Pentland, Sandy, 19, 26, 268

Performance, 97, 123, 147, 149, 154,
    197, 239

Peripersonal space, 208

Perlin, Ken, 135, 268

Perlin Noise, 135

Personality, 51, 129, 188

Perspiration, 34

Persson, P., 14, 268

PF Magic, 156

Pheromones, 34

Phonemes, 106, 235, 237, 238

Photorealism, 121

Photoreceptors, 102, 141

Physical Avatar, 209, 222, 224-228

Physical simulation, 14, 65, 66, 206,
    226, 227, 228

Physically-based modeling, 215

Pinocchio, 220

Pixar, 29, 71, 234

Point light displays, 130, 131

Pointing, 27, 36, 38, 53, 99, 110, 209

Pong paddle, 33

Post-human, 124, 258

Postsymbolic communication, 254

Posture, 27, 68, 93

Presence, 262, 269

Primates, 183

Procedural animation, 69, 152, 192,
    222

Proprioception, 34, 208

Prosody, 34, 240, 241, 247

Prosthetic, 55, 153

Proteus Effect, 148, 271

Prototype, 56, 70-72, 75, 76, 78, 152,
    156, 168, 200

Protozoa, 147

Proxemics, 60

Punctuation, 47-52, 55, 100, 101,
    106, 110, 241, 247, 269

Pupil, 70, 140

Puppet Strings, 66, 206, 220

Puppetology, 263

Ragdoll physics, 207, 221, 223, 227

Rapport agent, 41

Reich, Steve, 112

Renaissance Perspective, 198

Repliee, 118, 119

Retina, 182

Riel, Torsten, 207

Roberts, D. J., 201, 268

Robinson, Joanna, 44

Robots, 116

Rocket Science Games, 56

Role-playing, 144, 241

Rosedale, Philip, 222

Rotman, Brian, 24, 95, 113, 114, 269

Rubber Mask, 235

Rubik's Cube, 63

Saccades, 182, 183

Saldana, Zoe, 123

Salem, Ben, 76, 269

Sanskrit, 163, 258

Sarcmark, 50, 269

Schrödinger, Erwin, 210, 269

Schroeder, Ralph, 9, 73, 269

Second Life, 8, 11, 17, 18, 21, 30, 43, 69, 74, 86, 87, 94, 101, 124, 144, 145, 148, 154, 166, 167, 185, 191, 223, 237, 248, 267, 272

Seif El-Nasr, Magy, 18, 133, 265, 269, 270

Self-representation, 93, 94

Semiotics, 41

Sexual attraction, 34

Shemoticons, 30

Sheridan, Mary D., 23, 269

SheZoom, 30, 31

SIGGRAPH, 211, 266

Silicon Valley, 56, 206

Simlish, 165

Simon Fraser University, vi, 18, 133

Skype, 103, 201, 202, 247, 253, 256

SmartBody, 189

Smile, 16, 43, 45, 51, 52, 82, 109, 140, 144, 174, 218

Smileys, 9, 48, 50, 52, 55

Smooth-tracking, 185, 186

Snow Crash, 32, 269

Social gaze, 176, 180, 194, 248

Social Life of Avatars, 9, 269

Social networking, 30, 32, 100

Social signaling, 19, 26, 41, 93, 140, 177, 184, 247

Society of Mind, 208

Sociobiology, 35, 270

Sociometer, 26

Software interfaces, 55, 194, 260

Speech synthesizer, 22, 97

Speech-to-text, 99, 113, 240, 241

Sperling, Alan, 40

Sphere, 58, 59, 64, 103, 156, 208

Squeezils, 147

Stanford, 74, 121, 146, 263, 271

Stelarc, 154

Stephenson, Neal, 32, 269

Suler, John, 82, 269

Tail, 139, 141, 157

Tashian, Carl, 28, 269

Teeth, 113, 123, 235

Telekinesics, 22, 23

Telekinesis, 23

Telephones, 38, 103, 256

Text cursor, 33

Texting, 14, 175, 247

The Making of Second Life, 119

The Matrix, 88

The Sims, 101, 165, 234

The written word, 23, 24, 55, 98, 113, 129

There.com, 13, 15, 18, 46, 70, 71, 72, 80, 85, 87, 89-93, 123, 124, 152, 156, 157, 158, 168, 169, 171, 190, 200, 239, 248, 272

Third-person, 31, 57, 79, 81, 199

Tromp, J., 118, 269

Truss, Lynne, 48, 270

Tube metaphor, 108

Tufte, Edward, 47, 52, 270

Turing Test, 125-131, 133, 138, 241, 264, 270

Turk's Coffee Lounge, 36, 254

Turkle, Sherry, 10, 270

Twitter, 14, 103, 251

Typography, vi, 47, 48, 49

Uncanny valley, 116, 117, 119-121, 123, 124, 130, 132, 155, 208, 237, 238, 250

Understanding Comics, 117, 267

Unicode, 110

Unity Game engine, 134

University of Catalonia, 160

Uru, 90

User interface, 44, 51, 75, 175, 199, 223

User-generated content, 259

UTF-8, 110

Vancouver, 36, 111, 112, 133

Varela, Francisco, 108, 267

Verhulsdonck, G., 14, 29, 270

Vestibular, 62, 63, 208, 212

Vestigial Response, 142

Vicon, 131, 133, 148

Video camera, 95

Video Capture, 250

Video chat, 18, 22, 27, 101, 103, 104, 202, 247, 251, 263

Video conferencing, 27, 200-203

Virtual camera, 57, 79, 120, 199, 250

Virtual Dogs, 155

Virtual Embodiment, 55

Virtual environments, 31, 93, 101, 204, 262, 270

Virtual gaze, 78, 184, 189

Virtual human, 42, 69, 120, 189, 206, 207, 208, 222, 236, 266

Virtual reality, 15, 20, 57, 106, 107, 129, 146, 159, 211, 253, 267, 269

Visemes, 235

Visible Thought, 40, 262

Visualization, 117, 131, 176, 177

Voice chat, 16, 61, 88, 95, 99, 239, 241

von Károlyi, Catya, 37, 270

Vrba, E. S., 49, 264

Wagging, 138, 141, 142, 144, 146, 157, 158, 268

Wagner, James, Au, 119, 262

Weebles, 64

White, Michele, 184

Wii, 73, 260

Wilson, Frank R., 214

Wilson, E. O., 35, 139, 266, 270, 271

Winograd, Terry, 74

Winters, Catherine, 7, 8, 101

Woita, Susan, 15

Word-at-a-time, 173, 174, 248

World of Warcraft, 32, 43, 85

Worlds Away, 164

Worlds Chat, 61

Worthington, Sam, 123

WYSIWYG, 53

Yahoo!, 28, 173

Yee, Nick, 117, 118, 148, 271

Yilmaz, Emre, 147, 148

YouTube, 86, 100, 262, 267

Zamenhof, L. L., 28

Zeltzer, David, 215